SOLDIER

MISSION TO
ARGENTINA

OTHER BOOKS IN THIS SERIES

Available now at newsagents and booksellers

SOLDIER K: SAS

MISSION TO ARGENTINA

David Monnery

First published in Great Britain 1994
22 Books, Invicta House, Sir Thomas Longley Road, Rochester, Kent

Copyright © 1994 by 22 Books

The moral right of the author has been asserted

A CIP catalogue record for this book is available from the
British Library

ISBN 1 898125 14 7

10 9 8 7 6 5 4 3 2 1

Printed and bound in Great Britain by
Caledonian International Book Manufacturing Ltd, Glasgow

1

There had not been a silence so complete in the public bar of the Slug & Sporran since Rangers won an 'Old Firm' match at Parkhead in injury time. Every head in the bar was turned towards the TV, and every right arm seemed suspended between mat and mouth with its cargo of beer. On the screen the aircraft carrier *Invincible* was moving slowly out towards the Portsmouth harbour entrance, past quaysides lined with cheering, weeping, laughing, flag-waving crowds. The British were not just going to war; they were going in style.

James Keir Docherty could hardly believe any of it. He could not believe such rapt attention from a bar more used to toasting the IRA than the English overlord; he could not believe the Government was actually standing up to the Argentinian generals; and he could not believe his unit, B Squadron, 22 SAS Regiment, had merely been placed on permanent standby. Those lucky bastards from D Squadron were already on their way to Ascension Island, with G Squadron next in the queue.

At this moment in his life Docherty was even more disposed to military adventure than usual. A couple of miles away to the south, in one of the developments built on the grave of the Gorbals, his father was slowly dying of emphysema. And it looked like the old bastard was intent on taking with him any last chance of a meeting of minds between father and son.

Docherty was not needed at the bedside, that was for sure. His mother, his two sisters, half the block, probably half the city's trade-union officials, were all already there, drinking tea, swapping yarns, reliving the glorious defeats of the past. His father would be a candidate for best-loved man in the city, Docherty thought sourly. He would leave this earth on a river of good will, arrive at the heavenly gates with enough testimonials from the rank and file to make even St Peter feel inadequate.

He took the penultimate swig from his pint. The ships were still sailing out of the harbour, the crowds still waving. Every now and then the cameramen would find a particularly sexy-looking woman to zoom in on. Several seemed to be waving their knickers round their heads. Sex and death, Docherty thought.

He sighed, remembering those weeks on the beach at Zipolite, both bowed down by grief and lifted up by . . . by just sun and sea really, by the wonder of the ordinary. The best decision he had ever made, buying that air ticket; one of the few he had not regretted. 'My life's a fucking mess,' he murmured into his glass. A dead wife, a dying father, and he could not come to terms with either of them. Why the fuck hadn't they called up B Squadron?

Should he have another drink? No – getting pissed in the afternoon was never a good idea. Getting pissed alone was never a good idea. He drained the glass and got to his feet.

Brennan Street was wreathed in sunshine. A good-looking girl walking down the opposite pavement – long legs in black tights and big silver earrings dancing in dark red hair – reminded him how long it had been since he had had a woman. It was almost two years since his self-appointed mission to screw every whore in Glasgow had fizzled out in the near-bankruptcy of both pocket and soul.

It would be a while longer before he broke his fast, Docherty decided. He grinned to himself. He would go and see Liam McCall instead. After all, what else was religion but a substitute for sex?

He walked down Brennan Street, cut across Sauchiehall Street, and worked his way through the back streets to the Clyde. Every time he came back to Glasgow he was surprised by the speed with which it seemed to be changing, and mostly for the better. Sure, the shipyards were almost a memory, but new businesses seemed to be springing up everywhere, along with new eating places and theatres and galleries and leisure centres. There seemed to be so much more for young people to do than there had been when he was a boy.

But it was not all good news. The Gorbals of his youth – 'a jungle with a heart of gold' as one wit had named it – had simply been wiped away, and replaced by a desert. One without even the pretence of a heart of gold.

And unemployment was still going up and up, despite all the new businesses. If he had taken his father's advice when he was sixteen he would be on the scrap heap by now, a thirty-one-year-old with skills no one wanted any more. But would his father ever admit that? Not till fucking doomsday, he wouldn't. Joining

3

the Merchant Navy had been irresponsible, joining the Army something close to treason, getting into the SAS about as kosher as screwing Margaret Thatcher and enjoying it.

Why did he care what his father thought? Why was he in Glasgow when he could be enjoying himself at any one of a hundred other places in Britain? He knew he had made good decisions. His life was a fucking mess despite them, not because of them.

He crossed the river. At least he was in good physical shape, no matter what the state of his psyche might be. A couple of drunks were happily throwing up on the bank below. Two leather-jacketed teenagers with outrageously greased quiffs were watching them from the bridge and laughing. They had empty Chinese food cartons all around them, probably bought with the spoils of a mugging. A walk across Glasgow in the early hours of Sunday morning might be a good SAS training exercise, Docherty thought. Requiring stamina, unarmed combat skills and eyes in the back of your head. Not to mention a sense of humour.

Another couple of miles brought him to his friend's parish church, which stood out among its high-rise surroundings rather like the Aztec pyramid Docherty had seen half-excavated on the edge of Mexico City's central square. Father McCall, whom even the schoolkids simply called 'Liam', was standing on the pavement outside, apparently lost in thought. He looked older, Docherty thought. He was nearly sixty now, and his had not exactly been a life of ease.

'Hello, Liam,' he said.

The frocked figure turned round. 'Jamie!' he exclaimed. The eyes still had their sparkle. 'How long have you been back? I thought you'd be gone, you know, on duty or whatever you call it.'

'Duty will do. But no. No such luck. There aren't enough ships to transport all the men who want to go. I'm on twenty-four-hour standby, but ...' He shrugged and then grinned. 'It's good to see you, Liam. How are you? How are things here?'

'Much the same. Much the same.' The priest stared out across the city towards the distant Campsie Fells, then suddenly laughed. 'You know, I was thinking just now – I think I'm beginning to turn into a Buddhist. So much of what we see as change is mere chaff, completely superficial. And deep down, things don't seem to change at all. Of course,' he added with a quick smile, 'as a Catholic I believe in the possibility of redemption.'

Docherty smiled back at him. He had known the priest since he was about five years old. Liam would have been in his early thirties then, and the two of them had begun a conversation which, though sometimes interrupted for years on end, had continued ever since – and seemed likely to do so until one of them died.

'Do you have time for a walk round the park?' Docherty asked.

Liam looked at his watch. 'I have a meeting in an hour or so ... so, yes. 'And you didn't answer my question. How long have you been here?'

'I didn't answer it because I felt guilty. I've been here almost a week. My father's dying and ... well, I always seem to end up dumping all my problems on you, and, you know, every once in a while I get this crazy idea of trying to sort them out for myself.'

Liam grunted. 'Crazy is about right. Are you trying to put me out of business? How long would the

Church last if people started sorting out their own problems?'

Docherty grinned. 'OK, I get the message. You . . .' He broke off as a football came towards them, skidding across the damp grass. The priest trapped the ball in one motion, and sent it back, hard and accurately, with a graceful swing of the right leg. 'Nice one,' Docherty said. Maybe his friend was not getting old just yet.

'You know, it's a frightening thought,' Liam said, 'but I'm afraid I shall still be trying to kick pebbles into imaginary goals when I can barely walk.'

'Makes you wonder what sort of God would restrict your best footballing years to such an early part of life,' Docherty observed.

'Yes, it does,' the priest agreed. 'I'm sorry about your father,' he went on, as if the subject had not changed. 'Of course, I knew he was seriously ill . . . Is there no hope?'

'None. It's just a matter of time.'

'That's true for all of us.'

'It's a matter of weeks, then. Maybe even days.'

'Hmmm. It must be very painful for you.'

'Not as painful as it is for him.'

Liam gave him a reproachful glance. 'You know what I mean.'

'Aye. I'm sorry. And yes, it is painful. He's dying and I don't know how to deal with it. I don't know how to deal with *him*. I never have.'

'I know. But I have to say, and I've said it to you often enough in the past: I think he must carry more of the blame for this than you . . .'

Docherty scratched his ear and smiled ruefully. 'Maybe. Maybe. But . . .'

'Everybody loves him. Campbell Docherty, the man who'd do anything for anyone, who worked a twenty-hour day for the union, who'd give his last biscuit to a stray dog. One of our secular saints. He loves everybody and everybody loves him.'

'Except me.'

'There was no room for you, no time. Or maybe he just couldn't cope with another male in the family circle. It's common enough, Jamie. Glasgow's full of boys sleeping rough because their fathers can't cope with living with a younger version of themselves.'

'I know. I agree. But what do I *do*? It's nuts that I let myself get so wound up by this, I know it is . . .'

'I don't think so, Jamie. Fathers and sons have been trying to work each other out since the beginning of time. It's just something they do . . .'

Docherty shook his head. 'You know, every time I come back here I feel like I'm returning to the scene of the crime.'

'There's no crime. Only family.'

Docherty could not help laughing. 'Nice one, Liam.'

'Do you talk to him like you talk to me?' the priest asked.

'I try to. He even agrees with me, but nothing changes.'

'Maybe this time.'

'Maybe. There won't be many others.'

They walked in silence for a while. The dusk was settling over the park, reminding Docherty of all those evenings playing football as a kid, with the ball getting harder and harder to see in the gloom. 'Sometimes, these days, I feel like an old man,' he said. 'Not in body, but in soul.'

'Think yourself lucky it's only your soul, then,' Liam observed. 'It only needs one dark cloud coming in from the West, and every joint in me starts aching.'

'I'm serious,' Docherty insisted.

'So am I. But I know what you mean. You live too much in the past, Jamie . . .'

'I know. I can't seem to shake it, though. You know' – he stopped underneath a budding tree – 'there are two scenes which often come into my head when I'm not thinking – like they're always there, but most of the time they're overlaid by something more immediate. One is our parlour when I was a small kid. I must have been about six, because Rosie is still crawling around and Sylvia is helping Mum with the cooking, and Dad's sitting there at the table with a pile of work talking to one of the shop stewards, and I'm doing a jigsaw of the *Coronation Scot*. Remember, that blue streamliner? Nothing ever happens in this scene; it's just the way things are. It feels really peaceful. There's a kind of contentment which oozes out of it.'

'I remember that room,' the priest replied.

'The other scene is a style on a path up near Morar, for Christ's sake. I'm just reaching up to help Chrissie down, and she looks down at me with such a look of love I can hardly keep the tears in. Just that one moment. It's almost like a photograph, except for the changing expression on her face. It was only a couple of weeks later that she was killed.'

Liam said nothing – just put his hand on Docherty's arm.

'It's weird,' Docherty went on. 'I've seen some terrible things as a soldier. Oman was bad enough, but believe me, you won't find a crueller place than Belfast. I got used to it, I suppose. You have to if you're going to function. But sometimes I don't think I'll ever get over that room or that woman.' He turned to face the priest, smiling wryly. 'I couldn't tell this sort of thing to anyone but you,' he said.

'Most people couldn't tell it to anyone at all,' Liam said. 'You underestimate yourself. You always have. But I don't think you should put these two scenes of yours together. I think you will get over Chrissie, even if it takes another ten years. But that room of yours – it sounds almost too good to be true, you know what I mean? Like a picture of the world the way we want it to be, everyone in their proper place, living in perfect harmony . . .'

'Yeah. And what's even crazier: I know it wasn't really like that most of the time.'

'That doesn't matter. It can still be a good picture for someone to hold in their head. Particularly a soldier.'

'How did you get to be so wise?' Docherty asked him with a smile.

'Constant practice. And I still feel more ignorant every day.'

'Don't the Buddhists think that's a sign of wisdom?'

'Yes, but I have to beware the sin of pride where my ignorance is concerned.'

Docherty grinned. 'I think you're probably the most ignorant man I've ever met,' he said. 'And your time is up.'

The priest looked at his watch. 'So it is. I . . .'

'I'll drop by again tomorrow or the next day,' Docherty said. 'Maybe we can get to a game while I'm up here.'

They embraced in the gloom, and then Liam hurried back across the park. Docherty watched him go, thinking he detected a slowing of the priest's stride as he passed the kids playing football. But this time no ball came his way.

Docherty turned and began walking slowly in the direction of his parents' flat, thinking about the conversation he had just had, wondering how he could turn it into words for his father when the time came. Half the street lights seemed to be out in Bruce Street, and the blocks of flats had the air of prison buildings looming out of the rapidly darkening sky. Groups of youths seemed to cling to street corners, but there were no threatening movements, not even a verbal challenge. Either his walk was too purposeful to mistake, or here, on his home turf, they recognized Campbell Docherty's boy, 'the SAS man'.

His sister's face at the door told him more than he wanted to know. 'Where have you been?' she said through the tears. 'Dad died this afternoon.'

She was frightened for the first few minutes. The whole situation – sitting beside him in the back seat, her hands clasped together in her lap, watching the traffic over the driver's shoulder – seemed so reminiscent of those few hours that had devastated her life seven years before.

But this was London, not Buenos Aires, and the policeman beside her – if that was what he was – had treated her with what she had come to know as the British version of nominal respect. He had not leered at her in the knowledge that she was the next piece of meat on his slab.

That day it had been raining, great sheets of rain and puddles big as lakes on the Calle San Martín. And Francisco had been with her. For the very last time. She could see his defiant smile as they dragged him out of the car.

Stop it, she told herself. It serves no purpose. Live in the present.

She brought the crowded pavements back into focus. They were in Regent Street, going south. It was not long after three o'clock on a sunny spring afternoon. There was nothing to worry about. Her arrest – or, as they put it, 'request for an interview' – was doubtless the result of some bureaucratic over-reaction to the Junta's occupation of the Malvinas the previous Friday. Probably every Argentinian citizen in England was being offered an interview he or she could not refuse.

A vague memory of a film about the internment of Japanese living in America in 1941 flickered across her mind. Were all her fellow compatriots about to be locked up? It did not seem likely: the English were always complaining that their prisons were too full already.

Today was the day their fleet was supposed to sail. A faint smile crossed her face, partly at the ridiculousness of such a thing in 1982, partly because she knew how appalled the Junta would be at the prospect of any real opposition. The idiots must have thought the English would just shout and scream and do nothing, or they would never have dared to take the islands. Or they had not bothered to think at all, which seemed even more likely.

It was all a little hard to believe. The shoppers,

the late-lunching office workers, the tourists gathered round Eros – it looked much the same as any other day.

'We're almost there,' the man beside her said, as much to himself as to her. The car pulled through Admiralty Arch, took a left turn into Horse Guards Road, and eventually drew to a halt in one of the small streets between Victoria Street and Birdcage Walk. Her escort held the car door for her, and wordlessly ushered her up a short flight of steps and into a Victorian house. 'Straight on through,' he murmured. A corridor led through to a surprisingly large yard, across the far side of which were ranged a line of two-storey Portakabins.

'So this is where M hangs out,' she murmured to herself in Spanish.

Inside it was all gleaming white paintwork and ferns from Marks & Spencer. A secretary who looked nothing like Miss Moneypenny gestured her into a seat. She obliged, wondering why it was the English ever bothered to speak at all. It was one of the things she had most missed, right from the beginning: the constant rattle of conversation, the noise of life. Michael had put it all down to climate – lots of sunshine led to a street-café culture, which encouraged the art of conversation. Drizzle, on the other hand, was a friend of silence.

She preferred to think the English were just repressed.

A door slammed somewhere, and she saw a young man walking away across the yard. He looked familiar – a fellow exile, she guessed. In one door and out another, just in case the Argies had the temerity to talk to each other. She felt anger rising in her throat.

'Isabel Fuentes?' a male voice asked from the doorway leading into the next office.

'*Sí?*' she said coldly.

'This way, please.'

She walked through and took another offered seat, across the desk from the Englishman. He was not much older than her – early thirties, she guessed – with fair hair just beginning to thin around the temples, tired blue eyes and a rather fine jawline. He looked like he had been working for days.

The file in front of him had her name on it.

He opened it, examined the photograph and then her. Her black hair, cropped militantly short in the picture, was now past her shoulder, but she imagined the frown on her face was pretty much the same. 'It is me,' she said helpfully.

He actually smiled. 'Thank you for coming,' he said.

'I was not conscious of any choice in the matter.'

He scratched his head. 'It's a grey area,' he admitted, 'but . . .' He let the thought process die. 'I would like to just check some of the details we have here . . .' He looked up for acquiescence.

She nodded.

'You came to the UK in July 1975, and were granted political asylum in September of the same year . . . that was quick,' he interrupted himself, glancing up at her again.

'It didn't seem so,' she said, though she knew her father's money had somehow smoothed the path for her. She had friends and acquaintances who were still, seven years later, living in fear of being sent back to the torturers.

He grunted and moved on. 'Since your arrival you

have completed a further degree at the London School of Economics and had a succession of jobs, all of which you have left voluntarily.' He glanced up at her, as if in wonderment at someone who could happily throw jobs away in such difficult times. 'I presume you have a private source of income from your parents?'

'Not any more.' Her father had died four years ago, and her mother had cut all contact since marrying some high-ranking naval bureaucrat. 'I live within my means,' she said curtly.

He shrugged. 'Currently you have two part-time jobs, one with a travel agency specializing in Latin-American destinations, the other in an Italian restaurant in Islington.'

'Yes.'

'Before you left Argentina you were an active member of the ERP – the Popular Revolutionary Army, correct? – from October 1973 until the time of your departure from Argentina. You admitted being involved in two kidnappings and one bank robbery.'

'"Admitted" sounds like a confession of guilt. I did not feel guilty.'

'Of course . . .' he said patiently.

'It is a grey area, perhaps,' she said.

He smiled again. 'You are not on trial here,' he said. 'Now, am I correct in thinking that the ERP was a group with internationalist leanings, unlike those who regarded themselves as nationalist Peronistas?'

'You have done your homework well,' she said, wondering what all this could be leading to. 'I suppose it would do no good to ask who I am talking to?'

'I'm sorry,' he said, 'my name is Baldwin, Phillip Baldwin.'

'And you work for?'

'Oh, the Foreign Office, of course.'

'And what is this all about? Is the Foreign Office worried that the exile community is going to undertake a campaign of sabotage against the war effort?'

This time he did not smile. 'How do you view your government's invasion of the Falkland Islands, Ms Fuentes?'

'As just one more attempt to divert the attention of my country's people from their rulers' cruelty and incompetence.'

'Ah,' he said, twiddling his pen and looking out of the window. 'In that case, would you consider returning to your country to work for us?'

She was momentarily stunned. 'You mean as a . . . as a spy?'

'Yes, I suppose you could call it that.'

She half-laughed: the idea seemed so ludicrous.

Balwin seemed to take slight offence. 'Is it such a surprising request? You opposed that government once by force of arms. And it must have crossed your mind that defeat in this matter would probably finish the military as a political force for years.'

That at least was probably true. As was the reverse: victory would keep the beasts in power for the rest of the century. She looked across the desk at the Englishman, still idly twirling his pen. He was just going through the motions, she realized. He did not expect any Argentinian exile to agree to such a proposal, but someone somewhere in the bureaucratic labyrinth had decreed that they all had to be asked. As far as he was concerned, she would soon be walking away across the yard and another of her compatriots would be sitting in the chair answering the same questions.

'To spy on what?' she asked.

'That would depend,' Baldwin said slowly, stirring slightly in his chair. 'For the moment we are more interested in establishing a willingness in principle.'

'Are you offering anything in return for my services?' she asked.

His eyes narrowed. 'I think it would be hard to establish a real basis of mutual trust if remuneration was involved,' he said piously.

'Success would be its own reward,' she suggested sweetly.

'Something like that,' he agreed, with the faintest of grins.

'And if I wanted something other than money, like, for example, permanent residency visas for several friends?'

'That could probably be arranged.'

'I will consider it,' she said. The idea still seemed ludicrous, but . . .

Looking pleasantly surprised, Baldwin wrote down a number on his notepad, tore the sheet off and handed it to her. 'You can reach me on this number,' he said. 'Day or night.'

Isabel walked back to Piccadilly, phoned the travel agency with the news that she would not be back that day, and took a 19 bus to Highbury Corner. It was almost five o'clock. Her flatmate would probably not yet be home, but Isabel felt reluctant to risk having her thoughts interrupted by more instalments of the endless romantic soap opera which Rowan passed off as a life. She bought a cup of tea at the outdoor café in Highbury Fields and carried it across to one of the seats in the area barred to dogs.

For a while she just sat there and watched the world go by. Or rather, watched England go by. Since the meeting in Baldwin's office she had felt like she was living in an alien country. Which, of course, she was. It was just that most of the time the feeling was buried somewhere at the back of her mind.

'You must miss the heat,' people used to say to her when she first arrived. She had tried to explain that her birthplace in the far south of Argentina was just as cold and a lot windier than most of Scotland, let alone England, but nobody really listened. South America was jungle and gauchos and Pele and the carnival in Rio. It had to be hot.

She conjured up a picture of ice floes in the Beagle Channel, the wind like a knife, a beach full of penguins, the aurora australis shimmering in the southern sky. That was her home.

It was the one line, she realized, which had got to her. 'Would you consider returning to your country?' That simple question had somehow brought it all back. She had not been really unhappy in the prison of exile, not since the year or more of grieving for Francisco and of learning to live with what they had done to her. But she had not really been happy either, just endlessly marking time. The line from that Bob Dylan album of Michael's said it better than she ever could: 'And I've never gotten used to it, I've just learned to turn it off.'

That was her life – turned off. Friends, a lover, but no real comradeship, no real love. No purpose.

But could she really work for the English?

'My enemy's enemy is my friend,' she said softly to herself. 'Sometimes,' she added. Surely the Junta

17

would lose this war anyway, without her putting her own life at risk?

'If no one else will fight, then all the more reason for us to.' She could hear Francisco saying it, in the candlelit lodgings in Córdoba. They had just made love, and as usual he had been lying on his back, blowing smoke rings at the ceiling, surveying the world situation.

They had tortured and killed him, and maybe this was fate's way of giving her the chance to even the score. Maybe the wretched Malvinas had finally found a use for themselves, as a grave for the military's prestige. Defeat would bring a new government in Buenos Aires, one with untainted hands, one that could admit to what had been done to all those tens of thousands. Such honesty might bring the hope of redemption for her country. And for her.

'Don't cry for me, Argentina,' she muttered ironically.

She got up and walked slowly across the park to the flat she shared. Rowan was not home yet, and for once Isabel felt the need of some alcohol. An opened bottle of burgundy supplied the necessary, and she sat nursing a glass in front of the six o'clock news. The fleet was sailing out of Portsmouth harbour, flags flying, men saluting, loved ones waving. She remembered what Michael had said the previous evening, that no matter how much he despised the patriotism and the flag-waving, no matter how clearly he could see through all the sanctimonious crap, he had been appalled to discover that there was still a small part of him that felt somehow connected, even proud, of all this.

She had understood exactly what he meant, because

she knew that a small part of her wanted the English to fail in this war, wanted the beasts of the Junta to triumph in Argentina's name. And more than anything else, or so she later came to believe, it was the need to silence that small voice which led her to call Baldwin the next morning.

The next few days seemed more than a little unreal. She called in sick to her two jobs, perhaps not really believing that her new career as a Mata Hari would amount to anything. The Englishmen who were supposedly preparing her for her new career certainly did not inspire much confidence.

For one thing, it rapidly became clear to Isabel that they knew next to nothing about her country, either in the general sense or in terms of the current situation. What information they did have seemed to come from either the Argentinian press or American signals intelligence. The latter source offered great wads of information, almost all of which was rendered useless by the lack of any accompanying indication of the enemy's intentions. The newspapers, needless to say, offered only lies and conceits. It was obvious that British Intelligence had no one on the ground in Argentina.

Now, faced with the prospect of having someone, the Intelligence people seemed initially incapable of deciding what to do with her. Isabel could imagine them discussing the possibility of her seducing General Galtieri and learning all the Junta's secrets. Still, she did not fool herself into believing that they thought any more highly of her than she did of them. She was, after all, an Argie, a woman and a communist – which had to be three strikes and out as far as the Foreign

Office was concerned. If it was not for the fact that she was the intelligence services' only proof that they were doing anything at all that was useful, she would probably have just been sent home in a taxi.

It was on Friday 9 April, the day the other Western European countries swung into line behind Britain's call for sanctions, that some semblance of a coherent mission was offered to her. Baldwin escorted her through a maze of Whitehall corridors and courtyards to a spacious top-floor office overlooking St James's Park, and into the presence of a cadaverous-looking Englishman with slicked-back black hair and a worried expression. His name was Colonel William Bartley, but he wore no uniform, unless the City gent's pinstripe suit counted as one.

'We have thought long and hard about where and how you could be most usefully deployed,' he said, after the exchange of introductions and Baldwin's departure. 'And . . .' He stopped suddenly, sighed, and leaned back in his chair. 'I've read your file, of course,' he continued, 'and you wouldn't expect me to sympathize with your politics . . .'

'No,' she said.

'But of course, if these weren't your politics then you would not be willing to betray your own country on our behalf, so I can hardly complain.' Bartley grunted, probably in appreciation of his own logic. 'But you're obviously intelligent, and you can doubtless see our problem.'

She could. 'You don't want to tell me anything which I might turn over to my beloved government. Well, what could I say to convince you?'

'Nothing. In any case we are not merely concerned at the possibility that you will pass on information willing. There is always the chance you will be captured. And of course . . .' Bartley left the unspoken 'tortured' hanging in the air.

'I understand. And you are right – there's no way I would endure torture to save your secrets.' As I once did for a lover, she thought. 'So,' she said, 'it's simply a matter of calculating risks, is it not? The risk of my being a double agent, or of getting caught, against the risk of not telling me enough to make using me worthwhile.'

'Exactly,' Bartley agreed.

She stared at him in silence.

'You are from the south,' he said, 'which is useful from our point of view. How difficult would it be for you to set up shop, so to speak, somewhere like Rio Gallegos? Are there people who would recognize you? What sort of cover story could you come up with?'

'I come from Ushuaia, which is a long way from Rio Gallegos. I might be recognized by someone – who knows? – but not by anyone who would question my presence in the area. I could say I was looking up an old college friend . . .'

'Who is not there?'

'I did not know she had moved, perhaps?'

'Perhaps. Since you know the country and the people I will leave it to you, but I will give you one other suggestion: you are researching a travel book, perhaps in association with an American equivalent of that agency you work for, checking out hotels, local transport, things to see. It's a good excuse for moving around.'

'Perhaps.' She admitted to herself that it sounded a good idea. 'And what is my real motive for being there? The airbase, I suppose. You want to know

which planes, what armaments, the pilots' morale.'
She paused. 'And you'd probably like to know each
time they take off. Am I going to have to carry a radio
set into Argentina?'

'I doubt it,' Bartley said, obviously taken by surprise. 'How did you work all that out?' he asked.

'By reading the *Observer*. The British fleet was
created to operate in the eastern Atlantic, within
the defensive cover provided by shore-based aircraft,
and the one thing that scares the Admirals is their
vulnerability to air attack without such cover.' She
looked at him. 'Is this the secret you were afraid I'd
tell the Junta?'

Bartley at least had the good grace to blush. 'We
think the Super Etendards may be based at Rio
Gallegos,' he added, 'and doubtless the *Observer*
pointed out how concerned we are about the Exocets
they carry.'

'It did. But if advance warning is what you need,
surely it has to be by radio?'

'Perhaps. We have several weeks to worry about
that, and if it becomes absolutely necessary then one
can be brought across the border from Chile when the
time comes. First, we need to get you bedded in.'

For the next few days she was given an in-depth
briefing on military matters, at the end of which
she could not only recognize a Super Etendard by its
silhouette but also identify a wide range of military
equipment which might conceivably be *en route* to
the Malvinas from the Rio Gallegos airbase.

In the meantime her journey to Santiago – via New
York and Los Angeles on three separate airlines – had
been booked, her share of the rent on her flat paid six

months in advance, and four fellow exiles had been given reason to wonder at the sudden beneficence of the Home Office in allowing them permanent residence status. Rowan and her other friends had been told that she had been given a three-month commission to update tourist information in Peru and Bolivia. They were all suitably jealous.

Michael was also angry. Why had she not consulted him? Did she think she could behave in a relationship as if she was a single person? Did she care about him at all?

The answer to the last was: not enough. She liked him, enjoyed talking with him, found sex with him occasionally pleasurable but mostly just harmless fun. It was not his fault, and she would have felt sorrier for him if she believed he really loved her, but as it was . . . The last night before her departure, as she watched her nipple harden in response to his brushing finger and kiss, the bizarre thought struck her that she was like a ship which had been struck below the waterline, and that her captain had ordered the sealing of all the internal bulkheads, the total compartmentalization of the vessel. The rooms were all still there but she could no longer move from one to another. There were no connections. In the torture chambers of the Naval Mechanical School she had lost the pattern of her being, which was probably just a fancy description of the soul.

Her plane landed in Santiago de Chile at five in the morning on 19 April. According to the newspapers, the Junta's response to US Secretary of State Haig's peace plan was being conveyed to London, but no one seemed too sanguine about the prospects. According

23

to her own calculations, the British Task Force would be just over halfway to the Malvinas by this time. There was still between ten days and a fortnight before it came within range of the Argentinian Air Force.

The men in London had given her a new identity, albeit one very close to her own. She was now Isabel Rodríguez, a thirty-one-year-old Argentinian who had lived for several years in the United States, and who had never involved herself in the politics of her homeland. Later that evening, in her room at the Hotel San Miguel, she received the expected visitor from the British Embassy, a sallow, dark-haired man with wire-rimmed spectacles who looked distinctly un-English.

He introduced himself as Andrew Lawson. 'I am British,' he said apologetically, as if in the past doubts had been raised. 'I just look like a South American. Probably because my mother was Spanish. I have brought you the money' – he laid two piles of notes, one smaller Chilean, one larger Argentinian, on the bed – 'and the car is in the underground car park. A black Renault 5, AY1253S, in space B14. Have you got that?'

She nodded.

'I shall also be your contact in the south,' Lawson went on, taking a map from his pocket and unfolding it on the bed. 'See, this is Argentina . . .'

'I know. I was born there,' she said acidly. Maybe the Junta would win the war, after all.

'Ah, I'm sorry, of course. You know the south well?'

'I grew up in Ushuaia.'

'Ah, right. Do you know this road here, between Rio Gallegos and Punta Arenas?'

'I have travelled it many times, by car, by bus.'

'Good. What we need is a dead-letter drop – you understand? Somewhere where we can leave each other messages for collection. It should be on the Argentinian side, because the fewer times you have to cross the border the better. A stretch of empty road, a bridge over a stream, something like that.'

'It would be harder to find a stretch of road that isn't empty,' she said drily. 'Why must I cross the border at all?'

'A good question. And the simple answer is, I can't think of a safer way for you to let me know the location you've chosen. If you can . . .'

She thought about it 'You can't come to me?'

'I could risk it, but let's face it, I'd have trouble passing as a local at the border. I may *look* like a Latin American, but my Spanish isn't good enough . . .' He shrugged.

'A go-between,' she suggested.

'The fewer people know who you are the better.'

That made sense. 'OK, so I come into Chile . . .'

'To Punta Arenas. Your cover is a tourist guide, right? So you have to check out the local museums. There are three in Punta Arenas: the Regional Magellanes, the Patagonian Institute and the Salesian College. I'll be at the Salesian each Thursday morning from the 29th on.'

She looked at him. The whole business suddenly seemed completely insane. 'Right,' she said.

The road across the Andes was full of wonder and memories. Isabel had last driven it with Francisco in the early spring of 1973, when they had visited Chilean friends in Santiago, both of whom had perished a month or so later in the military coup. Then as now the towering peak of Aconcagua had shone like a beacon, sunlit snow against a clear blue sky, but then the love of her life had been with her, and the darkest of futures still bore a gleam of hope.

This time too she stopped at the huge Christ of the Andes, bought a steaming cup of coffee from the restaurant and walked up past the statue and its admiring tourists to where she could see, far down the valley, the distant green fields of her native country.

She had over 1000 miles to drive, and she planned to take at least three days, acclimatizing herself to the country as she travelled. That evening she stayed in Mendoza and, after eating in a half-empty restaurant, sat in the city's main square and listened to the conversations going on around her. Most of them seemed to be about the Malvinas dispute, and she found the level of optimism being expressed hard to credit.

The purchase of a newspaper helped to explain the high spirits. According to the Government, the British were bluffing – there would be no war between the two countries. Britain would huff and puff, but eventually it would come to its senses. After all, what nation would really send a huge fleet 10,000 miles for the sake of 1800 people? Though, of course, the editorial was swift to mention that, if by some mischance it really did come to a fight, then the armed forces of the nation were more than ready to do what was necessary for the glory of, etc, etc.

'Wrong,' Isabel muttered to herself, staring across the square at the vast wall of the silhouetted mountains to the west. There was no hope of the British coming to their senses, and consequently no chance that they were bluffing.

Isabel's sense of a nation with its head buried deep in the sand did not fade as she travelled south over the next few days. Everywhere she went she heard the same refrain: there would be no war. How could the British fight one so far from home? Why would they do so even if they could? There was no antipathy towards distant England; if anything, the old connection between the two countries seemed almost stronger for their mutual travail. Isabel was half-amazed, half-amused, by how many of her countrymen and women felt vaguely sorry for the British. It was almost pathetic, people told each other, the way the old country clung on to these useless relics of their past imperial splendour.

Her own state of mind seemed to be fluctuating more wildly with each day back in her native country. It all seemed so familiar, and pleasantly so, and it took her a while to realize that what she was reliving was her childhood and youth in the countryside, that memories of the city years with Francisco would need different triggers – the smell of San Telmo streets on a summer evening, book-lined rooms on a college campus, young earnest faces, a gun laid out in pieces on an oilskin cloth.

Each mile to the south took her further from those years, closer to the innocence which they had destroyed. Driving down arrow-straight roads across the vast blue-grey steppes of Patagonia seemed almost like a trip into space, cold and cleansing, more than human.

* * *

It was four in the afternoon on Saturday 24 April when Isabel reached the outskirts of Rio Gallegos. The town seemed much changed from when she had last seen it some ten years before. The oil industry had brought prosperity and modernity, along with a refinery which peeked out over the mostly brick-built houses.

The Hotel Covadonga in Avenida Julio Roca seemed to avoid the opposite extremes of ostentation and a clientele composed entirely of sex-starved oil workers. It was also centrally located and spotlessly clean. The manager proudly announced himself as Manuel Menéndez, and was surprised but pleased to learn that she intended to make a lengthy stay. Rio Gallegos was not usually noted for its tourist potential.

After a brief but enjoyable bargaining session over a reduced long-stay rate, Isabel explained about the guide book she was researching, and how the town was ideally located as a centre of operations. But perhaps, she wondered out loud, the trouble with the British over the liberation of the Malvinas had led the military to place temporary restrictions on the ordinary citizen's freedom to travel?

Not as far as Menéndez knew. There was no longer any civilian traffic from the airbase, and Navy ships were more often seen in the estuary, but nothing much else had changed over the last few weeks. The border with Chile was still open. 'It is all over, is it not?' he said. 'We have the Malvinas back, and I suppose we must thank the Government for that.'

Isabel agreed and went up to her room. After unpacking her meagre travelling wardrobe, she felt tired enough to lie down for a short nap. But her mind was racing too fast for sleep, and she soon decided that she should not waste the last hour of light in her room. Wrapped up in an extra sweater and her Gore-tex windcheater, she strolled purposefully down the Calle Rawson towards the estuary shore. Here she found that a new and pleasant park had been created along the river front. Many families were in evidence, the children already sporting their winter woolly hats. Over by the balustrade a group of young men in Air Force uniforms were enjoying a boisterous conversation.

She walked the length of the park along by the water. Two coalers were anchored in the mile-wide estuary, and beyond them the northern shore offered only a vista of steppe extending into the grey distance. As she turned to retrace her steps a growing roar lifted her eyes to the sky. A Hercules C-130 transport plane was coming in to land at the airport south of the city.

Back at the Covadonga, Isabel lay in the bath, thinking that any delay was likely to weaken her resolve. Wearing the dress she had brought with such an eventuality in mind, she went downstairs to the desk and asked Menéndez's advice. 'Where could she have some fun on a Saturday night?'

It turned out there was a big dance that evening at a hall in Calle Pellegrini. After eating a less than exciting dinner at a restaurant off the main square, she made her way across to the hall. At the makeshift bar there were several single women, presumably prostitutes, so Isabel kept her distance and tried to look suitably lost. It was not long before a middle-aged businessman's wife gave her the chance to tell her story: a single woman in a strange town, wanting some company but . . . She was soon adopted into their circle, a cross between a guest and a surrogate daughter.

She actually enjoyed the evening, and had almost despaired of it leading anywhere useful, when the party of Air Force pilots arrived. They were given a standing ovation, treated to free drinks and generally fêted as the nation's favourite sons. It did not take Isabel long to pick out her choice: he was tall and dark with a diffident manner and sad brown eyes. He looked as out of place as she felt.

His name was Raul Vergara, and fifteen minutes later they were dancing together, the rough serge of his uniform rubbing against her cheek. For one appalling moment she was back in the whitewashed room at the Naval Mechanical School, the lieutenant's swollen dick pushing against her obstinate lips, the smell of it mixed with the stink of fear that filled the building.

'You dance really well,' the shy young pilot whispered in her ear, breaking the dreadful spell.

2

The last slice of orange sun was disappearing into the western sea as the eight SAS men made their way across the deck of HMS *Hermes* toward the waiting Wessex helicopter. For the first time in many days the sky was clear and the ocean was not doing its best to tip the ship over. Maybe it was a good omen. But it was still bloody cold.

Each man was wearing camouflage gear from head to toe, with the exposed areas of the face painted to match. Somewhere in the bergen rucksacks slung across their backs, among the 90 lb or so of weaponry, communications equipment, medical kit and rations, each man was carrying the tubes of 'cam' cream he would need to freshen his make-up when the need arose.

They had split into pairs to check each other's cosmetic efforts before the final load-up. One of the two patrol commanders, Major Jeremy Brookes, had received five point eight for technical merit but only a minus score for artistic impression. He smiled through his mask at the thought.

Brookes's patrol, all of them members of G Squadron's Mountain Troop, were headed for the hills overlooking Port Howard on West Falkland, and none too pleased about it. 'But all the fucking

Argies are on East Falkland, boss,' Trooper Kenny Laurel had observed, with all the mildness of an articulated lorry.

'No, Hedge, they're not,' Brookes had explained, 'just most of them. And that's only as far as we know. The point of this exercise is to determine exactly where they are, every last one of them.'

'And where they're not,' Trooper Davey Matthews had observed.

'Thank you, Stanley. Besides which, someone had to draw the short straw, and it was us, OK?'

'Yes, boss.'

Admittedly, Brookes thought as he clambered aboard the Wessex, the straw no longer seemed quite so short. There might not be many Argies on West Falkland, but there was likely to be more than four of them. This was hardly a picnic they were embarking on. At the best it would probably consist of lying in a damp hole for days on end, bored out of their minds. He tried to remember who had said that a soldier's life was ninety-nine per cent boredom, one per cent pure terror. Was it Wellington? No, it was somebody else, but he could not remember who.

As they sat there waiting for the Wessex crew to appear – 'Fucking Navy were even late for the Armada,' someone observed – Brookes foolishly asked his seven co-travellers if any of them could remember.

'Genghis Khan?' a member of the other patrol offered.

'Nah, he said it was ninety-nine per cent terror,' someone corrected him.

'Bruce Forsyth,' Hedge suggested. 'What do you think, Mozza?'

Trooper David Moseley emerged from his reverie with a start. 'What?' he said.

'His mind's on other things,' Stanley said.

The little woman back home, I expect, Hedge thought. 'It drains your strength, Mozza, even thinking about them.'

'I was thinking about where we're going,' Mozza said, wondering guiltily whether not thinking about Lynsey at such a moment was something of a betrayal.

'We're all going to sunny West Falkland,' Hedge told him, 'where the beaches stretch golden into the distance and the hills are alive with the sound of sheep farting. We're all going on a summer holiday,' he sung, with a gusto Cliff Richard would have killed for.

So would their pilot, who had just arrived with the other two members of the crew. 'If you don't stop that horrible row Falkland Sound will be alive with your cries for help,' he said trenchantly.

'If you dropped him into Falkland Sound,' one of the other patrol noted, examining Hedge's undoubted bulk, 'it would probably drain it.'

'Then there'd only be one island to argue about,' someone else realized.

Major Brookes listened to the banter with half his mind, knowing it for what it was, a giddy chorus of nerves and apprehension. He still could not remember the author of his quote, and as he checked through his memory, another, less amenable one came to mind. He had first heard it from the lips of a dying IRA terrorist the previous year. Lying there, blood flowing freely from a neck wound into sodden leaves in an Armagh lane, the man had looked at him, smiled and recited: 'this is war, boys flung into a breach, like shovelled earth, and . . .'

He had died then, and it had taken Brookes many months to find the rest of the verse, and its source. Finally, the wife of an old friend had recognized it as a poem by the American Amy Lowell. He had looked it up and found the rest: 'and old men, broken, driving rapidly before crowds of people, in a glitter of silly decorations, behind the boys and the old men, life weeps and shreds her garments, to the blowing winds'.

These are the boys, Brookes thought, looking round at them: Mozza with his fresh-faced inno- cence, ginger-haired Stanley with his sleazy grin, the overwhelming Hedge.

At that moment the lights went out, the rotor blades reached a pitch which made conversation impossible, and the Wessex lifted up from the aircraft carrier's deck and started moving south-westwards, low across the South Atlantic swell.

Cecil Matheson poured himself a modest finger of malt whisky, took an appreciative sip and carried it across to the window. Through a gap between darkened buildings he could see light reflected on the Thames. In the street below he could see theatre and cinema-goers threading their way through the Saturday evening jam of taxis.

The buzzer sounded on his phone, and he took three quick strides across the room to his desk.

'Mr Lubanski is on the line,' his secretary told him.

'Mr Lubanski,' Matheson said jovially, wondering, not for the first time, why the American State

Department seemed to employ more Poles than the Polish Foreign Ministry. He had met this particular one on his last official visit to Washington, and been more impressed than enamoured of him. The fact that Lubanski was known to privately support a neutral American position *vis-à-vis* the current dispute only made the coming conversation more fraught with difficulty.

The lack of liking seemed to be mutual. 'Cecil,' Lubanski replied, with more familiarity but rather less enthusiasm. 'What can I do for you?'

'I'm sorry to take up your time at the weekend,' Matheson said with as much sincerity as he could muster at short notice. 'It's just a matter-of-clarification.'

'Uh-huh.'

'The President's speech on Friday . . .'

'The "ice cold bunch of land down there" speech?' Lubanski asked, a twist of malicious humour in his voice.

That was how Ronald Reagan had described the Falklands, and Matheson winced at the memory. 'Yes, that one,' he confirmed. 'Of course, we don't share the President's opinion in that respect, but we are . . .' He wanted to say 'glad that the US Government has at last realized its responsibilities to a NATO ally', but that would hardly be diplomatic.

'Pleased that we've finally fallen off the fence on your side?' Lubanski offered.

'That's certainly one way of putting it,' Matheson agreed, 'though I'd prefer to think you'd stepped down. In any case,' he continued hurriedly, 'we're obviously gratified by the sanctions announced by your Government, and by the President's promise of *matériel* aid. As regards the latter . . .'

35

'You'd like to know what's on offer.'

'Of course, but I'm sure that question can be handled through the normal channels. I have something more specific in mind.'

'Which is?' For the first time, Lubanski sounded vaguely interested.

Time to bite the bullet, Matheson told himself. 'AWACS,' he said. 'Airborne warning and control systems.'

'I know what AWACS are,' Lubanski said drily. 'And without putting too fine a point on it, I think I can safely say the answer will be sorry, but no.'

Like hell he was sorry, Matheson thought. 'Her Majesty's Government would like to formally request the loan of just two AWACS,' he pressed on.

'Like I . . .'

'If I could just continue,' Matheson said, rather more harshly than he intended, 'large British naval losses will hardly serve the interests of the United States. I'm sure I don't need to remind you that the Royal Navy's primary *raison d'être* is to safeguard the passage of American troops and armaments to Europe in the event of a major war . . .'

'No, you don't.'

'Then I fail to see the justification for a refusal of this request.'

'Bullshit, Cecil. You know damn well why we're refusing it. Put our own military into this little exercise of yours and twenty years of Latin-American policy goes down the tubes. You've already dragged us off the fence for the sake of 1800 sheep farmers, and now you want us to send AWACS planes? Are you sure you wouldn't like us to nuke Buenos Aires for you?'

Matheson took a deep breath, and swallowed the

temptation to tell Lubanski the best thing the State Department could do with its Latin-American policy was to tear it all up and start again. 'If we can't defend our ships against attacks from the mainland,' he said carefully, 'we may be forced to move against the source of the problem ourselves.'

'You mean bomb their bases? What with?'

'Vulcans from Ascension.'

For a few moments there was a silence at the other end. Then Lubanski, sounding more formal, replied: 'I think the British Government would be wise to examine the United Nations resolutions so far invoked, and particularly Article 51's definition of self-defence. I'm not at all sure that the United States would regard military action against mainland Argentina as falling within the scope of that definition. And, regardless of such legal niceties, I am completely certain that continued US support is contingent on a certain level of self-restraint in the British prosecution of the war.'

Another short silence ensued.

'You do realize how this looks from the British Government's point of view,' Matheson said eventually. 'You won't help us to protect our ships, and you won't allow us to protect them ourselves in the only way open to us. We've got young boys out there,' he went on, wondering whether sentiment would help, 'with next to no cover. And they're not fighting for sheep farmers – they're fighting against aggression, and for self-determination. I seem to remember,' he could not resist adding, 'that one of your presidents almost invented the phrase.'

'Before my time,' Lubanski said wearily. 'Look, Cecil, let me be as frank as I can about this. I personally think your war is a crock of shit, and I wouldn't have risked alienating a single Hispanic voter or a single Latin-American government to support it. I have colleagues who disagree with me, and who'd love to support the old country, you know, all that Ivy League shit. But even *they* wouldn't loan you a single airplane. It's just too much to ask. This is not our war – it's yours. You fight the damn thing with what you've got.'

'We intend to,' Matheson said, struggling to keep his voice level. 'Thank you for your time,' he said coldly, and hung up. He could almost hear Lubanski 3000 miles away, smirking about some Brit in a snit.

He shook his head to clear it, and poured out a more generous shot of whisky. He had, after all, got exactly what he had expected from the call. Nothing. And it would do no harm to make the Americans aware, privately, of how angry the British were with them. A measure of guilt might increase their generosity in other matters.

The real problem lay not 3000 miles away, but less than one. Matheson was almost afraid to imagine what alternatives to the AWACS were brewing in the Prime Minister's restless mind.

The flight took slightly less than a hour, most of it over the sea. Darkness had fallen, but despite the lack of a moon the Wessex crew had no trouble identifying the northern coast of Pebble Island on such a clear night. The Passive Night Goggles, or PNGs, which they had recently received from American sources, only came into their own when they were contour-chasing across the north-central part of West Falkland proper.

They set the Wessex down in a wide stretch of

desolate grassland. The ground looked hard enough, but for an instant seemed to give alarmingly. It was, Brookes thought, as he leapt down onto it, like landing on a springy pine-forest floor.

The other three followed him out, and the door closed on the grinning, waving members of the other patrol, bound for a similar mission further down the island. As arranged, Hedge moved off ahead to take up a defensive position on the slight ridge 100 yards to the east. The words 'So where's the fucking hotel?' floated back across the din of the helicopter taking off.

The others grinned, and Brookes examined the map and illuminated compass as the silhouette of the Wessex faded with the sound of its rotors. An almost eerie silence descended. I'm a long way from home, Mozza thought suddenly. At least there's no fucking wind, Stanley was consoling himself.

Hedge inched his eyes over the ridge line and suddenly came face to face with a dark and menacing shape. 'Baa-aaa,' it said. 'Kebabs!' Hedge whispered viciously.

They had been deposited just over 14 miles, as the crow flew, from their chosen site for an OP, or observation point, overlooking the small Argentinian base at Port Howard. Of course, there were no crows in the Falklands, and it was, as one of the SAS planners on *Resource* had observed, a bloody sight further as the penguin flew. The same terrain in, say, Wales, would not have been considered particularly difficult, but here the general dampness and usual high winds made everything twice as difficult.

The spongy ground often seemed as sapping as the Wembley turf in extra time, but occasionally it would either turn hard enough to jar every bone in the body or soft enough to swallow each foot in a clinging, gelatinous muck. The hills were not exactly steep, but large expanses of the slopes were strewn with flat rock slippery with lichen. And no matter which way you turned the wind always seemed to be blowing right in your face.

Given that this particular stretch had to be covered in relative darkness and near-total silence, with 90lb on each back and a less than perfect map, Brookes fully expected the journey to take two whole nights.

He told himself to look on the bright side. At least it was a clear night – no one was likely to walk off a cliff or trip over a sheep. And what had he joined the SAS for if not to experience moments like this, dumped behind enemy lines in a hostile environment with only a few good mates and his own wits to keep him alive, the stars shining bright above? At his age there would not be many more of them. The Falklands might not be Tahiti, but they sure beat the hell out of south Armagh.

They were walking in a staggered version of the diamond formation generally favoured by SAS four-man patrols on open ground at night. Stanley was out front, the lead scout, picking out the required route, with Brookes himself some 20 yards back and to the left. He was the navigational backup, and responsible for the patrol's left flank. Further back still, out to the right, Mozza was taking care of that flank, while Hedge was 'Tail-end Charlie', occasionally spinning round to check their rear. He was about 50 yards behind Stanley.

As was true of any SAS four-man patrol, each man had one or more of the four specialized skills: Brookes had languages and demolition, Stanley demolition and signalling, Mozza signalling, and Hedge medicine and languages. All but Stanley had some knowledge of Spanish, but there was not likely to be much call for it on this trip, unless they took prisoners. Or were taken prisoner themselves.

As an officer, Brookes was enjoying his second term with the SAS; in fact, his military career had become a series of alternating periods spent with them and his own parent regiment, the Green Howards. His first tour of duty with the SAS had involved active service in Oman and training secondments in two other Arab states, while the current stint, now nearing its end, had found him dodging bullets and bombs in Armagh's 'bandit country' and dispensing advice to local defence forces in several newly independent West Indian countries. Hairy it might be, and often was, but service with the SAS had been a great deal more interesting than service with the Green Howards, whom fate had given a less than fascinating peacetime role. War games in West Germany were a lot less fun than he had at one time imagined.

His wife, Clare, had preferred life with the Green Howards, in the days when she had still cared. Now, with both the boys at Shrewsbury and her own small business taking off, Brookes did not believe she even noticed which unit he was attached to. She was too busy scouring the Welsh Marches for the antiques she flogged off to her fellow-countrymen across the Atlantic. Their Hereford house looked more like a museum every time he returned from active duty abroad. Even the Spanish villa they shared with friends of hers seemed like a little piece of Hay-on-Wye.

He found it all hard to think about, and wondered

why he was doing so on a starlit stroll through the Argentinian-held Falklands. Where better? he asked himself.

He was not getting any younger – that was half the problem. Sure, he still had most of his hair, although no one would know it from the grey stubble which protruded skinhead-style from his head. And he was just as fit as he had ever been. But he was not Peter Pan, and maybe the bergen on his back did feel a bit heavier than it should. You could make up in experience what you lost in suppleness of limb, but only up to a point.

He was thirty-eight. What was he going to do in seven years' time, when his active career ran out? Fight for one of the desk jobs? Not bloody likely. But what else? He had always vaguely imagined that Clare would be there to share their old age. He knew it had been completely unfair, not to mention stupid – after all, what possible reason could she have for putting her life on permanent hold while he had fun? – but he had somehow expected that she would. Now when she bothered to write letters they were full of Stephen, her semi-partner. He was queer, of course – 'He's *gay*, Jeremy, not queer! – but then again, what did it matter whether or not she jumped into bed with the bastard: the point was that she obviously found him more interesting than her husband.

And then there were the boys. Total strangers to him, and he really had no one to blame but himself.

This was his real family, he thought, this bunch of highly trained lunatics. Men who could mention Genghis Khan and Bruce Forsyth in the same breath. Unfortunately it was a family with a cut-off date.

*　*　*

Up ahead of Brookes, Stanley paused for a moment to check the map against the reading on his illuminated compass. Satisfied, he resumed his progress across the sodden heathland towards the distant silhouette of a low hill, the M16 with attached M203 grenade-launcher cradled in his arms.

How, he wondered, could a man's mouth feel so dry in such a place? Walking across this island was like walking along the back of an enormous wet dog. He could feel the damp creeping up his legs and thought about the next few days of endless fucking misery in a damp hole. Worse than a Saturday morning in the West Bromwich Shopping Centre with his ex-wife.

The thought of Sharon cheered him up. With any luck she was having a worse time than he was since Brett — what a fucking name! — had been sent down for armed robbery. Stanley nearly laughed out loud. The prat had rushed into a local sub post office, waved a gun around, escaped with about fifteen quid, and then run out of petrol on the slip road to the M6. Brilliant! And this was the man she had left him for, the Inspector Clouseau of the West Midlands underworld.

Still, he had to admit she had been wonderful in bed. That tongue of hers would win the Olympics if they ever introduced it as a sport. He sighed. So it went. There were plenty more tongues out there.

And come to think of it, the hill ahead looked just like a breast. That was the trouble with the SAS: the old winged dagger was certainly a come-on in the pubs around Hereford, but wearing it seemed to involve long stretches of time in places like this where women were particularly thin on the ground. According to one of the sailors on the old 'Herpes', the members of

Scott's Antarctic expedition were away from women so long that they had started sleeping with penguins. 'Not right away, of course,' the sailor had said, 'and only heavy petting to begin with. They just kind of slipped into the habit.'

Stanley had not believed a word of it, of course. But he could understand that sort of desperation, he really could.

About 30 yards behind him, Mozza was snatching glimpses at the night sky between watching the men ahead and the empty country on the patrol's southern flank. This was undoubtedly the clearest night since his arrival in the South Atlantic, but the book he had brought all the way from England was back on the *Hermes*, and he was having trouble matching up his memory with the constellations filling the heavens above him.

Not that he supposed it mattered which was which. Though he had always liked the idea of the constellations, and as a kid often wondered who had first connected the dots and made them all up. After all, the stars in Orion did not actually suggest a hunter; it was possible to connect them up that way, that was all. In reality it was chaos, which was just as wonderful, and maybe even more so.

He glanced round to check that Hedge was still in sight behind him, then turned his eyes right again. It was funny: he had been really nervous in the helicopter, but now they were down on the ground and alone and in real danger he felt fine. He did not even feel homesick any more, though maybe he would once they got back to the ship.

Did the others feel like that, he wondered. Both

44

Hedge and Stanley had several more years than his twenty-three, and of course the PC was almost middle-aged. It was not just the years, either: sometimes he felt like a real innocent in their company, although there was no real reason why he should. There were not many tougher places to grow up than Manchester's Hulme estates, so he knew how to use the two great weapons of self-defence: fists and a sense of humour, and not necessarily in that order.

Sex was another matter. Stanley and Hedge hardly ever seemed to talk about anything else, but Mozza could not help wondering whether they actually enjoyed the act as much as the endless anticipation. According to Stanley there was only one difference between sex and an SAS mission – the briefing and debriefing came in a different order. And that was funny, and Mozza had laughed as hard as the rest of them, but it had nothing to do with real life or real people. When he was with Lynsey . . . well, it was magical. It was not a joke. And he would not dream of making it into one.

Maybe he was just lucky, he thought. He had often thought it. Maybe most people would not have wanted to grow up in Hulme but he would not have changed places with anyone. He supposed his family was poor by British standards, but only when it came to things, and even then, well, they had always had a TV. He had three sisters and two brothers, which had felt a bit too much at times, but they all got on, and being a bit cramped in the flat was probably what had started off the family tradition of spending each Sunday out in the country. That and the fact that his dad's job with British Rail got them a good discount on rail tickets.

And it had made him self-sufficient. It seemed strange maybe, but Mozza had thought a lot about this, about his ability to be alone in a crowd, to 'make his own space' as Lynsey put it, and he reckoned it was just something you had to learn as part of a big family in a small flat.

He thought about Lynsey. She was two years older than him, and had a kid already from her marriage to Jake. Mozza did not mind that at all: Hannah was a lovely kid and she seemed to like him. Jake had disappeared into thin air about two years ago, so it was hardly as if he was competing with anyone for the father role. And Lynsey . . . well, she was just perfect. She was kind, she was bright, she was gorgeous. And, after almost three months of intermittent courtship, she seemed to love him. He was a lucky man, all right.

The fourth man in the patrol was feeling rather less fortunate. Hedge – a nickname grounded in both his surname and the unruly tangle of wiry hair which graced his scalp – was suffering from periodic stomach cramps, and wondering what he had done to deserve them. Eaten navy food, probably. He hoped they were a passing phenomenon, so to speak, because in thirty hours or so they would all be sharing a small hide, and if he was still farting like this the others would probably insist on him giving himself up to the Argies.

He grinned in the dark and turned a full circle, peering into the gloom. There was nothing out there but wet grass and sheep, he thought. Life in the fast lane.

Maybe his stomach was feeling better. Maybe it

was just nerves. Hedge had seen enough action in Northern Ireland not to feel like a combat virgin, but he supposed being behind enemy lines was a reasonable enough place to feel nervous no matter how often you visited. Crossmaglen was bad enough, although you knew help was in calling distance. But this felt like being out on a limb.

People said the Argies would be poor soldiers, but he had seen their football team play, and *they* took no fucking prisoners, so fuck only knew how their Army would behave. Hedge was not keen to find out, not just yet. A day or so of acclimatization, that was what he needed, and a digestive system more at peace with itself. Then they could start throwing the bastards his way.

As often at times like this, he thought about his father, killed in a steelworks accident when Hedge was only fourteen. Although he knew it was stupid, he always wished his father could see him in this sort of situation, all grown up, doing something necessary and doing it well. His father had been a Labour man through and through, but he had also been a real patriot, and Hedge knew he would have felt really proud of England these last few weeks. And of his son.

What his father would have felt about an army career, Hedge was less sure, though from what he could remember getting out of the house and away from his wife and two daughters had been one of his dad's main aims in life. Joining the army had achieved a similar result for Hedge, and once he was in he had quickly found more positive reasons for staying a soldier. There had always been new challenges to drive him forward, right up to the ultimate goal of making it into the SAS. It had been a close-run thing on the Brecon Beacons – he had damn near given up – but the voice inside his head whispering 'I'll be so proud of you' had somehow pulled him through.

They marched on through the night, making frequent short stops to check their position and a couple of long ones to evade what turned out to be imaginary enemy patrols. About two hours before dawn Brookes decided it was time to dig in for the day. They had covered over two-thirds of the distance required, but the final quarter would bring them close to known enemy positions and called for a much more cautious approach. There was certainly no chance of completing the journey that night.

As it was, they were almost too tired to dig out the lying-up positions for use through the coming day. Brookes chose the western slope of a gentle ridge for their camp, and each man had the duty of digging out a large enough 'scrape' for himself, and making a roof for it with wire and turf. The excavated earth, which would be clearly visible to Argentinian pilots, then had to be removed from sight. Fortunately, a shallow stream ran down beyond the next ridge, and the soil could simply be spread along its banks.

As the first hint of dawn began to appear in the eastern sky all four of them were entrenched under their own camouflage roof, too tired to worry about the damp seeping out through the earthen floor of the scrapes. Brookes's last thought was 'so far, so good', while Hedge was thinking about the explosive properties of methane and Stanley was remembering his first time with Sharon.

Mozza was using the patrol's telescope through a

hole in his netting to watch the stars fade away in the east, and wondering how the hell he was going to stay awake for his two-hour watch.

Bryan Weighell, or 'Wheelie' as he had been known in younger days, briskly made his way through the various checkpoints separating the car park from his destination in the bowels of Whitehall. It was a sharp spring Sunday, sunny but far from warm, and he was still wondering what the hell he was needed for. It could not be anything to do with the teams inserted into East and West Falkland the previous night; all that was being handled through the usual channels. Starting in the ladies' lavatory aboard Resource, he reminded himself with a grin. He could still imagine Mike Phillips's face when the Navy told him that this was the SAS's floating HQ for the duration.

He wished he was there in person. They also serve who sit around and drink Guinness, he told himself. But it did not feel the same, not at a time like this.

In Conference Room B only one empty seat remained. The Prime Minister, whom rumour claimed had been known to punish unpunctuality with exile to one of the caring ministries, actually greeted him with a smile. What does she want, Weighell wondered.

'Lieutenant-Colonel Weighell, Officer Commanding 22 SAS Regiment,' she introduced him.

He acknowledged the various nods and half-smiles.

'Perhaps I should go round the table,' the PM decided. 'Cecil Matheson,' she began, smiling at the tall, patrician-looking individual on her left, 'Deputy Head of the Foreign Office and Chairman of the Joint Intelligence Committee.' On his left was Reginald Copley, a thin, grey-haired man who was apparently head of the Foreign Office's Latin American Desk. Last in line was the moustached Air Marshal Sir George Railton, Deputy Chief of the Defence Staff.

At the end of the table an arrogant-looking young man in a plain dark suit represented MI6. His name, hard though Weighell found it to credit, was Anthony Sharp. On the PM's right, between her and Weighell, sat Brigadier Mark Harringham, representing Fleet HQ at Northwood, and the imposing bulk of Dennis Eckersley, the Number 2 at the Ministry of Defence.

Seven men and one woman, Weighell thought. Seven professionals and one politician. Seven smelling of Old Spice and one of gardenia. He remembered a particularly disgusting joke about Snow White and her favourite Seven-Up. He told himself to snap out of it.

'We have a problem,' the PM began. 'Cecil?'

Matheson recounted the gist of his telephone conversation with the American State Department the previous evening, and though he made no overt criticism of the American decision to deny the Task Force AWACS assistance, he left little doubt in the minds of his audience what he thought of it.

The Prime Minister's stony face suggested to Weighell that she shared Matheson's irritation but had had enough time to suppress her natural instinct to express it. Maybe there was an inflatable model of Reagan hidden away somewhere in Number 10, on which she launched occasional assaults with her handbag.

'Do you have comments, Brigadier?' she asked Harringham.

'It's not good news,' he said mildly. 'I don't want to sound alarmist, but the AWACS were our last chance of going into action with even half-decent air protection . . .'

'Perhaps you could spell out the details, Brigadier,' the PM suggested. 'I doubt everyone here is fully aware of them.'

'Certainly. But there's nothing complex involved. Our ships in the South Atlantic are simply under-protected, particularly against the Super Etendards and their Exocet missiles. The Sea Dart missile systems on the Type 42 destroyers have no defensive efficacy against low-level attack. The Sea Wolf system, which does, is only mounted on the two Type 22 frigates. For air defence we have only the Sea Harriers, and there are pitifully few of them. In fact, there are only thirty-two Harrier airframes in existence. Once they're gone . . .'

'What about radar?' the MI6 man asked.

'Shipborne radar is notoriously ineffective in heavy seas,' Harringham said, 'and we have no airborne radar. This is not,' he added with an air of understatement, 'the war we were designed to fight. But . . .'

'Thank you, Brigadier,' the PM interjected. 'Very well, gentlemen. This is the problem we are here to discuss. There appears no way in which the Task Force can be certain of protecting itself, and I need hardly spell out the consequences if, say, one of the carriers were to be put out of action. In such an instance I don't think we could countenance the recapture of the islands. We would have no choice but to return with our tails between our legs. Another Suez, gentlemen. Britain would be a laughing-stock.' She glared at the company, as if daring them to imagine such an outcome.

'But,' she continued, 'there are other options. Mr

Sharp, would you like to give us an update on the intelligence situation within Argentina?'

Sharp almost preened himself, Weighell thought sourly. He had never had much time for intelligence types. As one of his friends had memorably put it: these were the boys at public school who tried to wank in silence.

'We now have an agent in place,' Sharp was saying. 'And we're expecting some useful information about the location of particular units, and about the sort of stuff the Argies are airlifting into Port Stanley.' He surveyed the table in triumph.

The PM ignored him. 'Is that it?' she asked Matheson. 'We have one man in Argentina?'

Our man in Argentina, Weighell thought irreverently, and, as it turned out, wrongly.

'It's a woman,' Matheson said coldly. 'I need hardly remind everyone here,' he went on, 'that the budget for what is called "humint" – human intelligence – has been cut to the bone in recent years, with most of the available resources going to the procurement of "sigint" – signals intelligence, of course – either from GCHQ or the Americans. It's an unfortunate fact of life, but like the Navy' – he glanced across at Harringham – 'the Intelligence Services have been organized with Europe in mind, not South America.'

The PM looked less than mollified. Weighell found himself idly wondering who would come out of this particular imbroglio with more egg on their faces: the Foreign Office, the Navy or the Intelligence Services.

'As a matter of interest,' the Latin American Desk man was asking, 'where is this agent "in place"?'

Sharp hesitated, caught the look on the PM's face,

and blurted out: 'Rio Gallegos – it's one of the two airbases closest to the Falklands . . .'

'But unfortunately not, as we had thought, the one with the Super Etendards,' Matheson admitted. 'It seems they are based at Rio Grande on Tierra del Fuego.' He reached into his briefcase, extracted a clear plastic folder full of photocopies of a map, and passed them round.

Weighell examined it with interest. He had spent so much time poring over maps of the Falklands that the mainland 400 miles to the west had more or less escaped his attention.

'Brigadier,' the PM asked, 'I take it that the destruction of these airfields and the planes based there would drastically reduce the vulnerability of the Task Force?'

'Of course.'

'Does the Air Force have the capacity, Air Marshal?'

'I would like to say yes, Prime Minister, but frankly I doubt it.' He looked round the table. 'Most of you probably haven't heard the news, but early this morning one plane dropped a stick of bombs on the runway at Port Stanley . . .'

There were murmurs of appreciation all round the table.

'It was an epic flight,' Railton conceded, 'and the psychological impact on the occupying force may have been worth something, but I'm afraid the military efficacy of the operation was rather more doubtful. Only one bomb actually hit the runway, and bear in mind that Port Stanley, unlike the Argentine bases, is known territory. Even more to the point, the Vulcan needed seventeen in-flight refuellings *en route*. I doubt if we could send more than one plane at a time against these two mainland bases. They'd be sitting ducks.'

'Thank you, Air Marshal,' the PM said coolly. On her left, Weighell noticed, Matheson was having a hard job concealing his relief. But the Foreign Office man had been conned, Weighell decided: the PM could not have been expecting anything else from Railton. Where was all this leading?

'One question,' the Latin American Desk man said. 'Since the Super Etendards and Exocets pose the main threat, could we not just move our agent in Rio Gallegos to Rio Grande and set up some sort of communication link between her and the fleet?'

It was an intelligent question, Weighell thought.

'It might be possible,' Sharp agreed, 'but it would certainly place the agent at risk. She has a good cover where she is, and promises to provide invaluable intelligence on the airlift. Agents are always more vulnerable when moved, and there would be the extra risk involved in getting the radio to her.'

Weighell suddenly knew where it was all leading, and why he was there.

As if on cue, the PM turned her beady gaze in his direction. 'Lieutenant-Colonel Weighell, how would the SAS like to have a crack at these airfields?'

Weighell noticed Matheson's eyes roll in horror, and resisted the temptation to let her steamroller right over him. 'If it's a feasible option,' he said, 'then of course we'd like nothing better.'

'Does it look like one?' she persisted.

Weighell imagined he was being given a major insight into how cabinet government worked in the modern age. 'I'm sorry, Prime Minister,' he forced himself to say, 'but I'd need a lot more data than I have now, not to mention a clearer idea of the task required. Are we talking about observation or military action here?'

'Either or both,' she said decisively.

'Prime Minister . . .' Matheson interjected.

'Hold on a moment, Cecil,' she said, patting him on the arm in as patronizing a manner as Weighell could remember witnessing, 'let's find out what we're capable of before you start explaining why we shouldn't risk it.' She turned a smile on Weighell.

You could rob a bank with a smile like that, Weighell thought. 'We're talking about two totally different missions,' he said. 'An attack on either airfield would require up to a squadron of men – around sixty that is – inserted from the air at night. Probably a high-altitude low-opening parachute drop. From a C-130.' He paused, gathering his thoughts. 'That in itself would not present any great problems, unless of course they were dropped into the middle of an Argentinian military base we knew nothing about. But there are always unknown hazards – the mechanics of insertion are simple enough.' As the bishop said to the actress, he thought to himself.

'The obvious problem,' he continued, 'would come with the extraction. Particularly if we're planning to hit two bases simultaneously. I don't see any way of getting two squadrons out, by air or sea. You'd need either every submarine in the fleet or, at that sort of range, every helicopter. And I presume the thought of 120 SAS men crashing across the border into Chile is hardly desirable, even assuming they could get to it . . .'

'God forbid,' Matheson muttered.

'What if the C-130 drops the troops and they secure

55

the airfields?' the PM asked. 'Surely then the planes could land and take the troops off?'

'It's theoretically possible,' replied Weighell. He had to admit a part of him was thrilled by the idea. The rest of him urged caution, however. 'For such an operation to be anything more than a suicide mission,' he went on, 'we'd have to know a hell of a lot more about the airbases in question.'

'Prime Minister,' Matheson interjected again, and this time she let him have his say. 'Such action . . .' he began, before pausing, apparently lost for words.

'Such action would have Washington in uproar,' she said. 'I know. Obviously we have no desire to upset the United States. Nor would it serve us well to do so, at least in the long run. But we have to balance such concerns against the well-being of the Task Force. Whether we like it or not, Britain's standing in the world is in their hands, gentlemen. I am not prepared to risk defeat merely for the sake of not offending a few American politicians. So please, Lieutenant-Colonel, I would like some contingency planning done. Just in case.'

'Very well, Ma'am.'

'Now, for the second possibility you mentioned – observation.' The basilisk stare transfixed him one more.

Here at least, Weighell felt on much safer ground. What the four-man patrols were already doing on East and West Falkland could just as easily be done on the mainland. Or almost. 'We could put two four-man teams down close to the two airbases,' he said, 'probably by Sea King helicopter, though I'd have to check the range-to-weight ratios. I would guess it would have to be a one-way trip. The terrain hardly lends itself to staying unseen, but that's just as true of the Falklands, and we already have patrols ashore on both islands.'

'If the trip in was one-way,' Matheson observed, 'you still have the problem of how to get the men out again.'

'True,' Weighell conceded. 'But eight men is a very different proposition to 120. One or two submarines could probably take them off. At worst, as few men as that could seek asylum in Chile without causing a major row.'

'My objections remain the same,' Matheson said. 'Of course I agree with you, Prime Minister, that we may have to take diplomatic risks for the sake of a military victory. Or at least to avoid a military humiliation. But I cannot see that the military situation at present is such as to justify this sort of operation.'

'Brigadier?' the PM asked Harringham.

'I cannot comment on the diplomatic issue, Prime Minister. Any improvement in the fleet's AEW capability would obviously be beneficial, but I am yet to be convinced that the enemy air force poses much more than a theoretical threat to the Task Force.'

'Dennis?' she asked.

'I would have to agree with the Brigadier,' Eckersley said. It was the first time Weighell could remember him speaking.

'Very well,' the PM said. 'I cannot say I feel entirely happy about it, but for the moment we shall shelve the idea of mounting mainland operations.' She paused. 'However,' she continued, turning to Weighell, 'I want detailed contingency plans prepared for those operations we have discussed. And I expect' – this time

Harringham was her target — 'the SAS to receive the full cooperation of the fleet in this matter. If and when something happens to tip the balance — if the threat to the Task Force does become more than theoretical — then I shall expect both a different consensus of opinion and the possibility of immediate action.' She surveyed those around the table — making sure she remembered who had been present, Weighell decided — flashed one wide smile at them all, rose from her chair and swept out through the door.

Around the table there were several heartfelt sighs of relief. Weighell found himself wondering whether sending the Junta a video of the meeting might not encourage an early surrender.

That same Sunday Isabel Fuentes drove out of Rio Gallegos in the black Renault 5 and headed south across the almost undulating steppe towards the Chilean border some 40 miles away. There was almost no traffic on the road: in the first 10 miles she encountered two trucks, one bus and about a dozen cars.

It was one of those late autumn days she remembered from childhood, clear but cold enough to make you think of the winter to come. On the seat beside her she had a vacuum flask full of coffee and a couple of spicy *empanadas* wrapped in a paper bag. Under the seat, sealed in a plastic bag, were the facts she had so far managed to accumulate concerning the military situation at the Rio Gallegos airbase. There were not many of them, but she had had only two meetings with her sad-eyed pilot, and all he had wanted to talk about was the girlfriend he had left behind in the north.

Which she supposed was both good news and bad

news. She had been prepared to sleep with him, at least on that first evening with the alcohol running through her blood, but she had also known that to do so would have marked a new low, a new stage in what felt almost like a self-imposed programme of dehumanization. On the negative side, her new status as a friend and confidante, though easier to live with, did not promise quite the same degree of mutual intimacy or trust. She had the feeling she could get him into bed with her, but was far from sure that her state of mind would survive such a level of pretence.

She was approaching the bridge she had chosen for the dead-letter drop. It was one of about ten such bridges in a three-mile stretch two-thirds of the way to the border. All of them were simple girder affairs, slung across dried-up streams. Presumably when the snow melted in the distant Andes they sent a swift current down to the Magellan Straits a few miles to the south.

The bridge Isabel had chosen had nothing to recommend it but the faded letters ERP, which someone had painted in fiery red a decade before.

Just beyond the bridge, she stopped the car, pulling over onto the dry gravel of the steppe, reached over for her vacuum flask and at the same time conveyed the plastic bag from its place under the seat to its new hiding place, stuck into her belt beneath the thick sweater.

She got out of the car, poured herself a cup of coffee and surveyed the road. It was empty for as far as she could see, which was at least a mile in each direction. She clambered down into the streambed, lifted out the two rocks she had previously chosen, and wedged the bag into the space. Then she replaced them, covering one corner of plastic with gravel.

The bag would not be found by anyone who was not looking for it. As a last safeguard she took the small plastic bottle out of her pocket and emptied its contents onto the dry earth beneath the bridge. After all, where else would a woman stop to urinate on such a road?

'You're really getting into the spirit of things,' she told herself wryly.

After sleeping in shifts through the daylight hours, Brookes's patrol set out once more, this time in a cross between drizzle and fog, to complete their journey. They were only a few miles from the coast of Falkland Sound now, and the signs of civilization, if sheep farming qualified as such, were thicker on the ground.

So too was evidence of the occupation. On one frequently travelled piece of ground – 'track' seemed too grand a word, 'road' a ludicrous exaggeration – signs of wheeled traffic had recently been overlaid by the marks of a tracked vehicle, presumably military. Halting for a moment's rest at a gate in a wire fence, Mozza bent down to check his bootlaces and discovered a discarded cigarette end of decidedly alien appearance.

'At least it proves we're on the right island,' Hedge whispered above the wind. 'You're a regular little Sherlock Holmes, you are.'

It also proved that the Argentinians were in the habit of passing in this direction, which increased the patrol's caution and slowed their progress still further. But they found no other sign of the enemy before reaching their destination on a hill a mile and a half north of Port Howard. They thought they could detect the faintest of lights where the settlement should be, but, with the rain not so much falling as hanging like a sheet of mist, it was impossible to be certain.

There was still about three hours until dawn, and Brookes allowed himself the luxury of a fifteen-minute exploration of the immediate area. In such conditions, he decided, it was almost impossible to pick out the best site for their hide with any certainty, and he was reluctant to undertake major earthworks twice. It was not a matter of the effort involved, but the virtual doubling of the chances that their interference with nature's handiwork would be spotted from the air. He told the men as much. 'We'll have to spent another day in scrapes,' he said. 'Behind this ridge line, I think,' he added, looking upwards. 'As far above the water-table as we can manage without unduly advertising our presence.'

'I think we'll need stilts to get above this water-table,' Stanley observed.

A few minutes later, in a sheltered hollow on the northern slope, they had found what Hedge pronounced to be 'the shallow end of the pool'.

'Why is it we're always getting into scrapes?' Stanley wondered out loud as they started digging.

3

Shortly before ten a.m. on Tuesday 4 April 1982, in the operations room of the Type 42 destroyer *Sheffield*, a blip appeared on the radar screen. Whatever it was seemed headed their way, and fast. Less than three minutes later, on the ship's bridge, the officer of the watch and the ship's Lynx helicopter pilot made visual identification. 'My God, it's a missile,' they exclaimed simultaneously.

A few seconds later the Exocet ripped through the ship's side, starting fires that proved impossible to control, causing the deaths of twenty-one men, and ultimately dooming the vessel to a South Atlantic grave. For the Task Force as a whole, the war had suddenly become real.

News of the catastrophe reached the British people seven hours later, at nine p.m. Greenwich Mean Time. Even the Ministry of Defence spokesman, who always looked and sounded as if he had been preserved in a cryogenic chamber since 1945, could not flatten the emotional charge of such news.

All those refrains of 'Britannia rules the waves' which had accompanied the Task Force's departure now came back to haunt the cheerleaders. Plainly the Royal Navy was in less than complete control of this particular stretch of ocean. The mindless glorification of slaughter which had accompanied the sinking of the *General Belgrano* two days earlier took on an even hollower ring. Were tabloid typesetters in Buenos Aires now arranging the Spanish equivalent of 'Gotcha!' for the next morning's front page?

More insidious still, for the first time the dread possibility of failure seemed to hover in the British air.

James Docherty watched the announcement on a pub TV somewhere in the middle of Glasgow, and felt for a few minutes as if someone had thrown a bucket of cold water over him. When it was over, when the news had been given, the analysis offered – all the usual crap – Docherty sat at the bar, beer and chaser barely touched, head in hands.

For four weeks now he had been floating in a drunken ocean of self-pity, anger and hopelessness. He was 'heading on down' he had told any stranger who cared to listen, 'just like the Task Force', floating further and further away from all those problems which could not be resolved by the heady mixture of modern technology and judicious violence.

Now, three hours into another magical mystery tour of Glasgow's bars, he took the destruction of the *Sheffield* very personally. That fucking Exocet had hit him too, he realized, ridiculous as it seemed. But it wouldn't sink him, oh no. In fact, it would wake him up. Or something.

He gingerly eased himself off the stool, wondering if his body had been as sobered by the news as his mind. It had not, but after an endless piss, his head leaning against the tiled wall of the Gents, he felt ready to face the night.

A chill breeze was blowing down Sauchiehall Street

from the east. Docherty leant up against a shop window and let the cold blast revive him.

After the death of his father he had asked for extended compassionate leave. They did not want him for the war, so what was the point of hanging out in Hereford listening to all the others bellyaching? In any case, he was not at all sure he had any desire to go back. And if the bosses could see him now, he thought, the feeling would be mutual. A faint grin flickered across his unshaven face, the first for a while.

Two men walked past, talking about the *Sheffield*, and brought it all back. Enough, Docherty told himself. This is as far down as you're going. Anything more would be fucking self-indulgence. In fact it already was.

'Who knows?', he asked himself out loud, as he walked back towards the dump he had been staying in, 'if things get bad down there, then maybe they'll need more of us.' It was not exactly likely, but if the call did come he wanted to be in some state to receive it.

Four hundred miles to the south the Prime Minister arrived back at Number 10 from the House of Commons. In the chamber she had sat there looking stunned as John Nott announced the ship's loss, but earlier that day, in the relative privacy of Number 10, tears had been more in evidence. Now she was entering the third phase of her reaction – anger.

'I want someone from Northwood – preferably Harringham – and Cecil Matheson,' she told her private secretary.

'You have the full Cabinet in the morning, Prime Minister.'

'I'm aware of that, Richard. I want Harringham and Matheson here now.' She started up the stairs, throwing 'please tell me when they arrive' back over her shoulder.

Matheson was still working at the Foreign Office, but Brigadier Harringham had to be pulled out of his bath and shuttled across from Northwood by helicopter. By the time of his arrival he had conquered his irritation – he could guess what kind of a day the PM had endured.

Once the three of them were gathered around one end of the huge Cabinet table she lost no time in coming to the point. 'Two days ago, Brigadier, you said, and I quote, that you were "yet to be convinced that the enemy air force poses much more than a theoretical threat to the Task Force". I take it the events of the day have changed your mind?'

'Sadly, yes,' Harringham said quietly.

'If it had been one of the carriers instead of the *Sheffield* we would now be in severe difficulties, would we not?'

'Yes.'

'Prime Minister,' Matheson interjected, 'obviously I do not want to minimize the potential dangers here, but I feel I must point out that the best intelligence we have suggests that the enemy only possesses five more of these missiles, and has next to no hope of procuring any more.'

She looked at him coldly. 'As you well know, Cecil,' she said with barely controlled hostility, 'our so-called "best intelligence" couldn't even forecast the invasion. You heard that chinless idiot the other day – we have one agent in Argentina, and even she's in the wrong place! The intelligence you're talking about is just sophisticated guesswork, and it isn't half-sophisticated enough for me to risk this whole venture on. I want some people in there, on the ground, counting the damn things. Or at the very least providing some sort of early warning for the fleet.'

Matheson could not ever remember seeing her so incensed, and for the first and only time in his life he could see the truth of the expression 'you're beautiful when you're angry'. He decided that resistance at this point would just increase her momentum. 'I agree that the new situation warrants the dispatch of one or two reconnaissance teams,' he said.

'Good,' the PM replied, thumping the walnut tabletop with the flat of her hand. 'So I can count on both of you to back me in this regard if it should come before the War Cabinet.'

'Yes, Prime Minister,' they said in relative unison, Harringham offering a sleepy counterpoint to Matheson's plaintive lead.

As the two men emerged into Downing Street, Big Ben was striking midnight. A mile to the east, in the Aldwych studios of the BBC World Service, a newsreader was announcing the loss of the *Sheffield*. Ten thousand miles away to the south, and three time zones away to the west, Mozza was lying in the patrol hide above Port Howard, listening in through headphones to London's plummy tones.

He could hardly believe it, and listened all the way through the news broadcast just to make sure he had got it right. Stanley and Brookes were out on a recce, but Hedge was snoring gently in another arm of the cross-shaped hide, and Mozza decided to wake him. This was the sort of news he had to share.

Hedge couldn't believe it either. Or at least did not want to. 'It was actually *sunk* – you're sure?' he said, his voice strained by the need to remain in a whisper.

'No, not sunk,' Mozza whispered back. 'They didn't say that. But it was hit by a missile, and everyone was taken off. The ship was burning. So maybe it has sunk by now. They didn't say.'

'Christ!' Hedge muttered. He could think of nothing more appropriate to say. Both of them lay there, looking up at their turf and wire ceiling, thinking the same thing: if the ships of the Task Force were being sunk, then how the hell were they going to get back home?

Rio Gallegos, 400 miles to the west, was awash with sky blue and white flags. As she walked across the central plaza to the Rakosi Bar, Isabel found herself in a swirl of deliriously happy people. The *General Belgrano* was forgotten, or at the very least avenged. It was as if all the doubts the Argentinians had silently nursed within their hearts through the weeks of wondering and waiting had finally and explosively been laid to rest. Let the English ships come! Our Air Force will send them to the bottom of the sea, each and every one of them!

Isabel could imagine the reaction in Britain to the news: there would be a sort of stunned disbelief. One of their ships had been *sunk*, and by *foreigners*! She found herself, not for the first time, feeling contempt for everyone involved in the whole

67

deadly farce – including, she had to admit, herself.

The atmosphere in the Rakosi mirrored that in the main square, only here the wine was offering additional lubrication to the festivities. She was greeted like an old and valued customer – something she was swiftly becoming – and invited to join in the toasts to the Air Force, the Navy, General Galtieri, Admiral Anaya, Mario Kempes, even Eva Perón.

She thought it unlikely that Raul would turn up that night – he was probably celebrating with his comrades out at the airbase – but resisted the temptation to return to her hotel just in case. Three glasses of wine worked their magic, and she was both celebrating with the best of them and watching herself from some hidden vantage point with barely restrained disgust.

Raul's arrival probably saved her from making a fool of herself, though how dangerous a fool she would luckily never know. He seemed to have had more than a few drinks himself, and insisted on taking her for a walk through the riverside park. His arm grew tighter around her shoulder, and when they turned at the end of the promenade to retrace their steps he pulled her to him and kissed her passionately, his beery breath almost turning her stomach, his right hand pressing at her left nipple as if it was a doorbell.

'Raul, no,' she said without thinking, and tried to disengage herself. She felt both nauseous and suddenly sober.

He leaned down to kiss her bare neck.

'Think about your Mariella,' she said softly.

'Ah, Mariella!' he said dramatically, and dropped his head on her shoulder. To her surprise he started shaking.

For a few minutes Isabel gently stroked his head as he clung to her. 'Come, let us sit down,' she said eventually.

He allowed himself to be led to one of the wrought-iron seats overlooking the darkened estuary.

'Tell me about it,' she said.

He gave her a half-laugh, half-sob, then wiped the tears away from his face with an angry sweep of the back of his hand. 'How can I tell you?' he asked. 'How can I tell anyone? You will just think I am a coward. I . . .' He looked at her imploringly. 'One of us sinks an English ship, and suddenly we are all heroes, but . . . we are . . . today Juan Morales was lost – I didn't really know him, but every day one of us is killed, every day . . .' He grabbed her arm. 'I am so afraid I will never see Mariella again,' he said.

'You will,' she replied. What else could she say?

Raul just shook his head. 'Another one of us dies and we are all celebrating because of the English ship,' he said. 'It's not just me,' he added, almost belligerently. 'Everyone is afraid.'

'Are the English so powerful?' she asked.

'No, it is we who are weak. We have so few missiles, and hardly any spares if the planes are damaged. There are so *few* of us. And the Army is sending boys to the Malvinas – I see them lining up to take the flight across each night and they are *boys*. We have experienced soldiers. Why are they not being sent to fight?'

'I don't know,' Isabel said, though she could make a good guess. They would be needed to protect the Junta from the people if and when it all went wrong.

The day after the sinking of the *Sheffield* dawned clear and cold, as if trying to make up for the gloom it had engendered in the SAS hides scattered across the two main islands. For the first time since their arrival eighty hours before, Brookes's patrol had a clear view of the landscape around them, and in particular the small settlement of Port Howard below. Similarly, this would be the enemy's first chance to see them.

Despite this threat, Mozza found himself more taken by the landscape than the apparently sleeping enemy garrison in the settlement below. The two night marches across endless swathes of peat, rock flats and wet tussock grass, had conjured up a rather boring picture of the islands, which the days of mist and fog had only served to reinforce. But here were the silver-blue waters of Falkland Sound beneath a pure blue sky, and the distant hills of East Falkland rising in subtle shades of green and brown between them. A flock of birds was drawing graceful patterns in the air above the water, and the randomly scattered handful of buildings which made up Port Howard seemed supremely insignificant, no match at all for the vastness which surrounded them.

It was weird, Mozza thought. This was what the war was all about, yet it seemed much further away here than it did among the Task Force. He reluctantly tore himself away from such thoughts, and back to the job in hand, jiggling the veil into position so as to prevent any tell-tale reflection, rearranging his legs within the cramped hide, and aiming the telescope at the settlement below.

It was strung out between the foot of the hill and a narrow inlet, which was itself separated from the Sound proper by a long peninsular no more than 200 yards wide. A couple of small boats were bobbing at anchor in the inlet, but there was nothing bigger — no fishing vessels and no enemy naval craft.

The settlement seemed to boast five actual houses, but there were three times as many buildings, including two large corrugated sheds, which Mozza assumed were normally used at some stage of the process whereby sheep were turned into either lamb chops, pullovers or both. To the south of these, and partly obscured by them, an acre or two of almost flat meadow had been adopted as a camp-site by the invaders.

Mozza counted the tents — there were just over 200. Reckoning four men to a tent, and taking into account that the officers had probably installed themselves in the available buildings, he thought the garrison must number about 1000 men. They had no artillery as far as he could see, and only two vehicles were visible: one jeep and a half-track armoured personnel carrier — probably the one whose trail they had come across on their second night's march.

He wrote down his observations, and was about to record the lack of air support when the drone of a distant helicopter insinuated its way into his consciousness. He watched it draw a lazy arc across the Sound, and then descend gingerly onto an area which had obviously been cleared with that purpose in mind, the grass waving wildly in the rotor's wind. Two figures climbed out, both in uniform. One was a lieutenant, the other, to Mozza's surprise, a general. They walked out from under the still swirling blades and paused, as if uncertain where to go next. Then they moved on across the grass towards the nearest clump of buildings.

On the near side of these, hidden from the new

arrivals, another couple of officers were hurrying in their direction. One was still apparently fastening his trousers.

'Morning crap took longer than expected,' Mozza murmured to himself. He looked at his watch. It was almost seven – time to wake Stanley. He wrote down the time of the arrival, the type of helicopter – a Huey UHIH – and the ranks of both the visiting officers and their reception committee. He took one more look through the telescope, and found the pilot standing up against his machine, having a piss. After a vigorous shake the Argentinian turned round and strolled a few yards away across the meadow, lighting up a cigarette and gazing around at the scenery with an obvious air of self-satisfaction.

'What's he thinking about?' Mozza muttered to himself. The wife back home? The wonders of nature? Or was the Argie a city boy, wondering what the fuck he was doing in the middle of nowhere? At that moment, as if he sensed the watching eyes, the man looked up towards the distant OP, stared for a moment, then turned away, taking another drag on his cigarette.

Mozza put down the telescope and used his unaided eyes for a quick panoramic sweep of the hillside. The four of them had decided, after a long, whispered discussion on their third night ashore, to plant themselves in this immense stretch of bare slope precisely because it gave them such a field of vision. In daylight at least there was no chance of their being surprised, and the freedom to talk without fear of being overheard was a priceless asset when it came to retaining one's sanity.

The downside of such an exposed OP was the lack

of any cover, or any other lines in the landscape which might draw the eye away from signs which the patrol had inadvertently left on the 'surface'. They had turned themselves into hostages of their own camouflaging skills, and only time would tell if they had occasioned some slight change in texture or colour only visible from the air.

At night, of course, none of the above applied. They were safe from the air, but the risk of an enemy patrol passing nearby was ever-present, so that strict silence had to be maintained at all times.

So far the only loud and inadvertent sound they had made was an enormous snort from the sleeping Hedge. That had been two nights before, and the rain had either covered the noise or deterred the Argentinians from venturing out on patrol. According to Stanley, the wind had been blowing the wrong way for the snort to be heard on the mainland 400 miles away.

Mozza remembered this as he worked his way back through the cramped space towards the gently snoring trooper. In response to his shake the ginger-haired Brummie's eyes opened with a start, only to wearily close once more when they saw who it was.

'Where's the luscious Conchita?' Stanley murmured.

'Which luscious Conchita is that?' Mozza asked.

'The one in my dream,' Stanley said sleepily. 'You're too young to hear the details. All I can say is that she brought her own Angels' Delight.'

It was raining in Hereford. It seemed to Lieutenant-Colonel Bryan Weighell to have been raining all day, the dark-grey skies adding their sombre voice to the general depression which the previous day's news had spread across the Stirling Lines HQ of 22 SAS Regiment. Even his tea was cold. He pressed his intercom to demand a fresh cup, and was informed that Major Neil Strachan had just arrived to see him. 'Make that two teas then,' he said. 'And a couple of rock cakes,' he added.

The red-haired, blue-eyed Neil Strachan came through the door with a smile on his face and a briefcase in one freckled hand. 'Rock cakes,' he echoed, in an accent straight out of the Great Glen. 'We *are* taking risks today.'

'I hope you've come to cheer me up,' Weighell observed.

Strachan sat down. 'That depends on what you find cheering. I've got the preliminary report you asked for. You've got a general map, I take it?'

Weighell lifted up *The Times Atlas* which had been leaning against one end of his desk, placed it between them and opened it where he had left the bookmark: Plate 121 – Argentina, Chile, Uruguay.

'That'll do for the wider picture,' Strachan said. He pulled a couple of smaller maps out of his briefcase. 'You wouldn't believe how hard it was to find more detailed maps. This one' – he was opening a 1:1,000,000 map of Argentina's Santa Cruz province – 'comes from the Bodleian Library, and I got this one' – it was a 1:500,000 map of Tierra del Fuego – 'from an outdoor activities bookshop in Covent Garden.'

'What are the Task Force using?' Weighell wondered out loud.

'God only knows. Probably old school atlases. Anyway . . .'

He was interrupted by the arrival of two steaming mugs and two ominous-looking rock cakes.

'I think I'll pass on the grenades,' Strachan said. 'I still haven't found the last filling they ripped out.'

'You don't know what you're missing,' Weighell said, taking a giant bite. 'Now what have you got?'

'Right. Let's start with the first idea, of dropping two squadrons onto their airbases to commit general mayhem. It's a non-starter, Bryan. I could tell you why in detail if you want, but it seems like a waste of time. It would just be a suicide mission to end all suicide missions. We'd probably lose less men using the Harriers in a kamikaze role.'

Weighell grunted. 'That's what I thought from the word go,' he said, 'and I think the PM thought so too . . .'

'I thought it was her idea . . .'

'It was. I think she just threw it into the pot so it would look like a concession when she plucked it back out again.'

'Makes sense,' Strachan agreed.

'But the other idea . . .'

'Is not so mad. In fact, it makes a lot of sense, if you ignore any diplomatic ramifications. Let's start with the job itself.' He placed his two maps side by side over Weighell's atlas. 'The terrain's far from perfect, mostly because there's no cover to speak of . . .'

'Like the Falklands.'

'Exactly. And since we already have patrols concealed above their bases on the islands there's no real reason why we shouldn't do the same on the mainland. Here and here' – he used the end of his pen to point out a particular spot on each map, one a few miles south of the Rio Gallegos airbase, one between the latter and the sea – 'seem like reasonable locations given the limits of the maps available to us. I would put in a request for American satellite photos, but that would rather give the game away and . . .'

'No, don't do that, not yet anyway.' Weighell was studying the two maps. 'And the idea would be to land them 20 miles or so away, as on the islands?'

'Maybe nearer. Maybe even farther away – I'll come to that in a moment. But one last word on the job itself: there's no technical problems I can see. They can send out the info in burst transmissions on a Clansman, which should minimize the chances of interception. Of course, if the Argies have any sense they'll be mounting patrols, but if they weren't then our lads could just sit there with their telescopes and have a picnic. There's bound to be some risk.'

'Ah, that reminds me,' Weighell interjected, the last chunk of rock cake poised perilously between plate and mouth. 'I've been trying to get some guidelines from Whitehall about our lads' status if they should be caught. Without any success, of course. There's been no declaration of war – there never is these days – so even if they're in uniform, and I'm still assuming they will be, then it's rather in the lap of the Argentinians.'

'Who don't exactly inspire confidence,' Strachan said soberly.

'No. And in any case the politicians are just as likely to insist the lads are not in uniform, so that they can wash their hands of them . . . I don't know . . .' He scowled. 'Let's leave it for the moment.'

'Right,' Strachan said. 'Getting them there. I don't have any cast-iron information, but from what I've gathered so far it seems that a one-way trip by a Sea King is the best bet.'

'It couldn't get back?'

'Not a chance. Which of course creates its own problem: what do we do with the Sea King once it has delivered its passengers, and even more to the point – what do we do with its crew?'

'What about the HALO option?'

'We don't think so. The consensus of opinion is that it would be much harder to get the men in unobserved that way. We think the Argentinian radar defences are too good for anything other than a low-level insertion. High-altitude, low-opening tactics won't do.'

'OK, so assuming you can render a Sea King and its crew invisible how do we get the patrols out again?'

'That shouldn't be a problem. One of the submarines will pick them up at two designated spots.'

Weighell took a gulp of his tea and found it had already gone cold. 'Under that cynical façade, do I detect a certain enthusiasm for this venture?' he asked.

Strachan took the question seriously. 'Yes, I think it could be done,' he answered. 'And should be,' he added almost as an afterthought. 'It *is* the sort of mission the regiment was designed for.'

'Well, the PM is certainly in favour,' Weighell said drily. 'Who do you have in mind for the magnificent eight?'

'Ah. Well, there's one obvious difference between the Falklands and Argentina . . .'

'One of them belongs to us?'

'In Argentina they speak Spanish. Of course, we hope the need for conversation doesn't actually arise, and that we can get in and out without a single "*buenos días*", but just in case something goes wrong it would be nice to send eight Spanish-speakers.'

'Are there that many in the Regiment?' Weighell asked incredulously.

'There are eight that we know of,' Strachan said. 'And would you believe that three of them are this moment sitting in an OP above Port Howard on West Falkland: Major Brookes and Troopers Laurel and Moseley?'

'Where are the other five?'

'Here in the UK. Two are from A Squadron, the other three from B. The B Squadron bunch have worked together before: an undercover mission in Guatemala during one of the Belize scares.'

'Sergeant Docherty,' Weighell remembered.

'Yes. His father died a month ago, and he's on compassionate leave, but the time's almost up.'

'He had all that time off when his wife died.'

'Yes, almost six months.'

'Why so long? I was in Oman at the time,' he added by way of explanation.

'Because they thought he was worth it,' Strachan replied. 'He's a damn good soldier.'

'This isn't just the Scots' Old Boys Network talking?'

'You must be joking – the bastard's a Celtic supporter.'

Weighell laughed. 'OK, you have him earmarked as PC. What about the others?'

'The other two Spanish-speakers in B Squadron are Wilkinson and Wacknadze. The two in A . . .'

'I would think six out of eight was good enough, Neil. If you've got two four-man patrols who know and work well with each other, then go with them.'

'Right.'

'Of course, it'll mean pulling Brookes's bunch out

of West Falkland,' Weighell added. 'All that bracing fresh air,' he mused. 'Have you called the others in?'

'Not yet.'

'Do it. By my reckoning they'll be sending the Marines ashore in less than three weeks from now. And by that time our job should have been done. We're on borrowed time, Neil.'

The mountain with which he shared a surname was wreathed in cloud, but Stewart Nevis – 'Ben' to his comrades in the SAS – had his eyes to the ground as he walked moodily up Fort William railway station's single platform. The conversation he had just had with his girlfriend was still going round and round in his head, and the temptation to go back for more was a strong one. But he would see her again the following day, and Morag would be none too pleased if he turned up again at the shop. The tourist season might be hardly started, but she took the division between work and play as seriously as she took everything else. They had wasted her lunch hour arguing, and that was the end of it until tomorrow.

He looked once more at the front page of the paper he was carrying, emblazoned with news of the catastrophe which had befallen the *Sheffield*. It was hardly the day to ask him to choose between the Army and her, Ben thought. But she had.

This should be an easy choice, he told himself, one eye on the Class 37 engine backing up the relief track, diesel fumes pumping into the grey sky. He loved Morag, and the SAS was just a job.

But it was more than that. Why could she not understand? Or maybe she did. Maybe she understood it better than him, which was why she was forcing him to choose.

'I won't marry a soldier,' she had said. It was as simple as that.

He had asked her what she expected him to do instead. His elder brother Gavin would take over the family farm, so there was no place for him there, at least not in the long run. And new jobs were not exactly thick on the ground around Fort William. So what did she expect him to do?

'Anything,' she had said. 'You could do anything. What's the good of what you're doing now?' she had asked, neatly changing the subject, he now realized. At the time he had been too busy defending himself.

'How often do we have a war?' she had asked. 'Once in a blue moon. And when we do have one half of you get left at home . . . oh, I know that's not your fault, you idiot, but don't go giving me all that nonsense about duty. You're in the army because you love it.'

Which was true enough, Ben admitted. The engine was being coupled up to the Mallaig train: it was time to get aboard.

He sat gazing out of the window as the train rattled through the junction and struck out for Banachie and the bridge across the Caledonian Canal. Outside his window Loch Linnhe stretched away to the south; on the other side of the train mountain slopes clambered towards the clouds.

His uncle had driven engines on this line from the beginning of the fifties through to his death from a heart attack in 1981. He had never really come to terms with diesels: the old steam engines, he had always said, were like women – you could always coax that little bit more out of them, particularly with a little tenderness. A few years later he had decided that women had changed as much as engines: these 'uppity-tight' modern women, as he called them, were just like diesels – one little problem and they just cut out altogether.

Morag was not like that, Ben thought. If anything she was a bit old-fashioned, even by Fort William standards. But then that was one of the things he loved about her.

She had said she was prepared to wait a year or so for Ben to make up his mind. There was no hurry. But in some strange way – as if the decision had nothing to do with him – he was impatient to know which way he would jump. He could not honestly imagine relinquishing either Morag or the SAS, but he seemed to have little choice.

At Arisaig he got down from the train and started down the lane towards the family farm. The sky was clearing in the west, and 10 miles away across the water Eigg was bathed in sunlight, but he still felt oppressed by his dilemma.

His mother was in the kitchen, rolling pastry for an apple pie. She glanced up as he came in, a worried look on her face. 'There's a message for you,' she said. 'It's by the phone.'

Ben went through into the living room, and read the note in his mother's neat writing. He had been ordered back to base.

'Is it the Falklands?' his mother asked from the door. Her voice was calm, her eyes full of anxiety.

'No idea,' he said.

Darren 'Razor' Wilkinson was also talking to his mother, though the view through their back-room window was somewhat different: a half-tamed garden and the backs of terraced houses in the next street. Out of sight between them, but distressingly loud all the same, trains on the Barking to Gospel Oak line ran through a brick-lined cutting.

'Who are you going out with tonight?' she asked from the armchair. She already had her uniform on for the night shift at Whipps Cross Hospital.

'Her name's Corinna – but then nobody's perfect.' He gave the sleeve one more stroke of the iron, and turned the shirt over.

'Where did you meet her?'

'You're not going to believe this,' he said, 'but in a vegetarian restaurant. A future one, that is.'

'You mean, that lot down the street who are doing up the place on the corner? I was thinking of offering them a hand, if I ever get a spare ten minutes.'

'Like mother, like son,' Razor said.

'You offered to help?' she asked disbelievingly.

'Not exactly. You remember Rick Manning? Well, he knows them from the Tap & Spile, and one of the women . . .' He grinned. 'He fancies her. So he volunteers both himself and me for a morning's hard labour.' He smiled at the memory. 'Nice people, though. For do-gooders, anyway,' he added slyly.

'And Corinna – is she a do-gooder?' his mother asked sweetly.

'I hope she'll do me good.' He leaned over and pulled the plug out of its socket. 'I'm going for a bath while you watch *Emmerdale*,' he said.

Upstairs, he tuned the radio to LBC in the hope of hearing some news of Spurs, did his best to extend his lanky frame in the short bath, and wondered how the evening would go. He hated first dates – it was always so hard to just be yourself.

He thought about Corinna. She was attractive enough – blonde, no more than verging on plump, a lovely smile – and she certainly seemed bright. Not that a degree usually impressed him, not in itself anyway. He thought most people would benefit from three years of freedom to read books and talk to each other without any irritating need to earn a living.

But if there was one thing he had learnt at school it was that the bright ones usually saw through everything a little too quickly for their own good. It was the plodders who went to university, them and the ones whose parents never considered any other possibility.

Fuck 'em all, he thought. He considered the possibility of fucking Corinna. She would be all cool and collected, he reckoned, the sort who neatly folded her clothes on the chair and lay there with the sheet up to her neck, waiting for you to pull it down.

Hmmm, he told himself. Down, boy.

It would be a fun way to spend a night, all right. But not, he suspected, much more.

It was a definite handicap, he decided, having a mother who was more interesting than his girlfriends. He could not understand why she had not found someone for herself – she was attractive, clever, had lots of interests, and was as nice as you could find. You would think there would be a queue of men stretching down the street.

He knew she had stayed single on purpose until he left home, but that was nearly six years ago, and she was not getting any younger. Maybe she was too interesting, and scared them off. He was convinced she wanted someone. It was such a lonely life when he was away, which was most of the time. And she worked so bloody hard for next to nothing. It made him angry just thinking about it. Fucking government.

He got out of the bath, dried himself and went downstairs in the Spurs dressing gown she had made him ten years before. The phone was ringing.

'Yes, he's here,' his mother said, handing him the receiver.

His orders were the same as Ben's. 'I'm afraid Corinna has missed her chance,' he said mildly.

Nick Wacknadze examined the prints on the walls of his host's home and sipped at the glass of wine Brendan had poured for him. It was not bad, and probably expensive: Brendan seemed like the sort who would enjoy demonstrating that he had a degree in yuppieology.

Not to mention modern art: none of the prints seemed to bear any relation to the world Wacknadze lived in, and they all seemed to be by men whose names began with M. Miró seemed to be a child, Munch someone who badly needed a good laugh, and Matisse was obviously colour-blind. Modigliani sounded like an ice-cream. Picasso, who at least had a name which began with another letter, must have felt pretty chuffed to make so much loot with such a bad squint. What a fucking con it all was.

'Are you interested in art?' Brendan asked, appearing at his shoulder like a wraith. He made the question sound like sympathy, as if it were impossible for someone like Wacknadze – a *soldier*, for God's sake – to appreciate any of civilization's finer points.

Wacknadze felt like hitting him, but that was not the

sort of response which would please his wife, Anne, busy chatting in the kitchen to Brendan's wife, Judy. The two women had met in pre-natal classes the year before, which was why he was enduring this particular 'dinner party'.

'I'm more into music,' he said.

'Oh. What kind?'

He's probably expecting me to say Abba, Wacknadze thought. Some kind of Celtic folk music was dribbling out of their hosts' expensive sound system, so he decided to take a chance. 'Early classical, Bach, medieval church music,' he said, and enjoyed watching Brendan's jaw drop a millimetre. And he really did have an interest in those kinds of music; he just never seemed to get the time to pursue it. The last time he had got an album of Gregorian chant from the library Anne had asked him whether it was playing at the right speed.

'Dinner's ready,' Judy said from the doorway, and the two men went through to the other half of the through lounge, where a walnut dining table occupied pride of place. Anne smiled up at him, but not as warmly, Wacknadze thought, as she smiled at Brendan. A glimmer of suspicion flickered across his mind.

He looked at Judy, wondering if she seemed aware of anything. She didn't. But she was not half as attractive as Anne, Wacknadze thought.

She was a better cook though, he thought, tucking into the meal. The other three were talking about the local housing market, a topic which proved easy to exhaust.

'As an Army man, how do you see this whole Falklands business?' Brendan asked after a long lull.

'In what way?' Wacknadze asked carefully.

'Well, don't you think the whole business seems a bit disproportionate? Sending an enormous fleet down there just to save a few hundred sheep farmers. It would be cheaper to pay them each a million pounds and hand the whole lot over to Argentina.' He laughed at his own acumen.

It would be cheaper, Wacknadze thought, but not in the way Brendan was using the word. 'I don't think you can put a price on principle,' he said shortly, hoping someone else would change the subject.

'Which principle do you mean?' Judy asked.

'That an aggressor shouldn't be allowed to get away with it.'

'OK,' Brendan agreed, 'but we're always letting them do just that. When the Russians invaded Afghanistan we didn't do anything.'

'There was no way we could do anything.'

'Exactly,' Brendan triumphantly. 'So this is not a matter of principle at all – we're only going to war with Argentina because we can.'

Did his host really believe this shit, Wacknadze asked himself. 'The way I see it,' he said, 'it's very simple. Those people want to be British – every last one of them – and if we *can* stop them being taken over by another country then we should.'

'You don't think Argentina has any case at all?'

'Nope. And even if it did, this is not the time to say so. We lost a ship yesterday, and a lot of men.'

'They lost a lot more men a couple of days ago.'

Wacknadze smiled. 'Well, they started it.'

'I don't . . .'

'Brendan, why don't you open another bottle,' Judy

said, 'and let's talk about something more cheerful, shall we?'

The rest of the evening passed smoothly enough, with Wacknadze leaving most of the talk to the other three, and trying to ignore both the sharp looks from Anne and the glow on her face when she listened to Brendan.

In the car on the way home she was first silent, then angry. 'Why were you so rude at dinner?' she wanted to know. 'There is more than one way to look at the world, you know.'

'You mean, I should learn to see both sides?' he asked sarcastically.

'It is generally considered a sign of maturity,' she said.

'Fuck maturity,' he said. 'Some of my mates are probably going to get killed out there, and you want me to feel sorry for Argentina? Jesus Christ, you can't send soldiers into a war and expect them to see both sides.'

'You mean, you have to wear blinkers before you can start killing people,' he said coldly.

He wanted to hit her, but she was driving. And by the time they got back home he just wanted to see the back of the whole fucking evening. He paid the babysitter her usual exorbitant fee and let her out the front door.

'Oh, by the way,' the girl said, just as she was about to shut the door, 'there's a phone message for you in the hall. Something about reporting in first thing in the morning.'

Another day would have helped, Docherty thought, examining himself in the toilet mirror. His eyes had lost their rusty edges, but his face still seemed almost preternaturally pale. He looked like a fucking ghost.

In fact, he thought, weaving his way back down the aisle to his seat, he looked even worse than he felt. Which was both good and bad, depending on which way you looked at it. Good because it meant it would not take that long to regain his usual fitness; bad because the bosses might think he was not up to whatever they had in mind for him.

He hoped to God it involved travelling a long way from Glasgow – the moon might just be far enough. Though wherever it was, as long as he had something to keep mind and body occupied it would be fine. The Falklands would be just dandy. Spitzbergen would be great. The only place he did not think he could stand was Belfast, and all those bloody hours sitting in cars both bored out of your skull and hyper-aware that someone might just walk up and blow your skull away.

If they ordered him there he would tell them to shove it, he thought, surprising himself with the vehemence of the feeling. Was he really ready to throw thirteen years of Army life out the window? Maybe he was.

And maybe not. He did not really know how he felt. He had held himself tight as a vice until his father's funeral, then taken to the drink with a vengeance. Neither form of existence had allowed for much in the way of feeling, which he supposed was why he had embraced them. Now, sober enough to feel the inside of his head shaking, he needed a third way of avoiding himself. Like playing cat-and-mouse with the Argentinian army on the Falklands.

The train was pulling into Preston. The old Ricky

Nelson hit ran through his head: 'I'm a travelling man, made a lot of stops, all over the world . . .' And he had. The Arabian desert, the mountains of Oman, Hong Kong, Belize and Mexico. 'And in every port I own the heart of at least one lovely girl . . .'

He had only ever owned the heart of one, and he had never been outside Britain with her. He was twenty-six, and Chrissie only eighteen, when they first met, at an exhibition of Islamic architecture in Edinburgh. Docherty fell in love with the graceful minarets and domes during his time in Oman, and he fell in love with her in front of a large photograph of Tamerlane's mausoleum in Samarkand. 'A soldier's tomb,' he said out loud, not realizing she was behind him.

'You must be one yourself,' she said with that simple directness she applied to everything and everyone.

'Is it that obvious?' he asked.

'My dad was one,' she said by way of explanation.

They had coffee together, then a walk in West Princes Street Gardens and a meal at an Italian restaurant on Castle Street, talking all the time. He admired her quickness and her knowledge, loved her sense of humour, felt almost intimidated by the loveliness of her face. He could hardly believe she could have any real interest in him. But at Waverly Station, where she came to see him off on the last train back to Glasgow, she returned and amplified his goodnight kiss, and agreed to meet him again the following weekend.

Three months later they were married. Another six months and she was dead, knocked down by a car on a zebra crossing less than 100 yards from their Hereford flat.

Docherty had not known what to do. For several

weeks he ranged the streets of Hereford and the surrounding countryside like a wounded dog, both pathetic and dangerous. Then one day he suddenly realized he had to get away – it did not matter where. He went into a library, opened an atlas at random, and found himself looking at a map of Mexico. He cleared his bank account and bought a return ticket – Mexico refused to admit travellers without one – and told his mates he was off. They managed to persuade him that compassionate leave would look better on his record than desertion, and for another twenty-four hours, while the formalities were gone through, he managed to hold himself together. The next day he was airborne, and that same evening he was strolling across Mexico City's central square, still in turmoil but somehow out of danger.

Over the next few months he travelled all over the country, staying in cheap hotels and eating in cheap cafés, falling in love with Spanish architecture as he had with Islamic. Chrissie was always with him, occupying a space in his heart and mind which nothing could apparently touch, but the rest of him slowly came back to life, reflecting the brightness of the Mexican light and landscape.

After five months he felt the country and the travelling way of life had done everything for him that they could. He began to hunger once more for his old, disciplined sense of purpose – that sense of service which he knew came from his father, but which he had offered to first the Black Watch and then the SAS. In any case he was running out of money.

He returned to Hereford and, somewhat to his surprise, was taken back into the regiment's fold. In the five years that had since passed neither he nor they had found any reason to regret the decision, but neither had Docherty learned to reopen Chrissie's mausoleum in his heart.

One day he would, Liam McCall had told him, but he was not so sure. He had always thought that one day he would come to terms with his father, but now he could only come to terms with not coming to terms. Or something like that. The bastards kept widening the goalposts. Jesus, he thought, I could do with a drink.

Fortunately the buffet bar was closed. The train was gliding through Warrington: in another twenty minutes it would be at Crewe, where he hoped there would be a connection for Shrewsbury and Hereford. Once the wait had only been ten minutes, but once it had been six hours.

This time they split the difference, and it was three. He watched the sun rising behind the Shropshire fields, silhouetting the mass of the Long Mynd, ate his breakfast of Mars bar, Pepsi and crisps between Ludlow and Leominster, and did his best to make himself look less dead than alive as the train rolled the last few miles into Hereford.

A cab took him to the Stirling Lines barracks in Redhill, where the orderly sergeant informed him that he was expected in the 'Kremlin' briefing room at 0900 hours. 'Christ, you look dreadful,' he added sympathetically.

It was only eight-forty: there was time for a proper breakfast. Docherty stowed his gear in his empty locker and made his way to the canteen, where three familiar faces already had their snouts buried in the trough.

'It's the boss,' 'Razor' Wilkinson announced.

'Welcome back, boss,' 'Wacko' Wacknadze said seriously.

'Ben' Stewart just smiled.

'And they promised me a new team of comics,' Docherty told the woman behind the servery, as he collected eggs, bacon and toast and a large mug of tea. 'A funny one, this time.'

She pursed her lips in sympathy.

'So where's the rest of B Squadron?' he asked the others as he sat down.

'All in the bosoms of their families,' Razor told him, 'except for Banjo – he's in detention for assaulting a parking meter in the High Street last night.'

'What did he assault it with?' Ben asked.

'The ultimate blunt instrument – his head. Some civilian wound him up about the war – about his not being down there – so Banjo charged him like a bull, and the other bloke just stepped out of the way . . .'

'Like a bullfighter,' Ben murmured.

'Exactly. And the bull head-butted a parking meter.'

Docherty could not help grinning.

'Anyway, boss,' Razor went on, 'to answer the unstated part of your question – we four are the only ones who've been called back. Which seems a bit weird. I mean, they're hardly likely to be chartering a C-130 just to send us down south, are they?'

'Maybe they'll stick us in with supplies or something,' Wacko observed.

'Oh great. Us four and a Hercules full of toilet rolls for G Squadron. But why just four of us? And why us four?'

'Spanish,' Ben suggested. 'You three all speak it, and they probably reckoned I was needed to make sure you didn't get lost.'

92

'With your map-reading skills we should take a sundial,' Razor said.

'All will be revealed in about five minutes,' Docherty said. He thought Ben was probably right about the Spanish, and that, coupled with the fact that only four of them had been summoned, suggested something very interesting indeed. 'Come on, let's get over to the Kremlin.'

They were the first to arrive, not counting the mounted water-buffalo's head which had surveyed the room since the regiment's Malayan days. It looked even more pissed off than usual, Docherty thought. Or maybe it was just him. He had probably needed more than the hour's sleep he had got.

'You look terrible, boss,' Razor told him.

'I know,' Docherty grunted. He closed his eyes, but only for a few seconds. Footsteps behind him announced the arrival of Lieutenant-Colonel Bryan Weighell and Major Neil Strachan.

'You look awful, Docherty,' was Weighell's first comment.

'Just a long train journey and no sleep, boss,' Docherty said brightly.

'If you say so. Anyway, good morning, gents. This is not a normal briefing – you'll be getting that on the *Resource* – but . . .'

'Does that mean the Task Force, boss?' Docherty asked.

'Yes, I'm sorry, I'm jumping the gun . . .' He noticed that all four men were grinning at him. 'I'm glad to see you're all eager to go,' he said, 'but don't get too carried away – this is a volunteers-only mission, and we want you to think seriously about what you're letting yourself in for before you volunteer.'

I was right, Docherty was thinking. It had to be the mainland.

'Neil here will give you the bare bones,' Weighell said.

Strachan got up to stand beside the map which had been hung in front of the blackboard. 'It's very simple,' he said. 'Even you lot should be able to understand it. Here are the Falklands' – he pointed them out – 'and here, more or less, is the Task Force. As you no doubt know, it has no air early warning system, and the perils of being taken unawares were demonstrated only too clearly the other day. The *Sheffield*,' he added unnecessarily. 'The Exocets are our major concern, but we're not even completely sure at which of these two airfields' – he pointed out Rio Grande on Tierra del Fuego and Rio Gallegos on the Argentinian mainland – 'they are stored. The Task Force needs advance warning of flights from both, and the plan is to put two four-man patrols ashore, one to monitor each airbase. They will report take-offs as they occur, thus giving the fleet about four times the warning they are getting at present.' He paused. 'It's hard to exaggerate how important such an increase in warning time could be. It could save one of the carriers, and that might mean the difference between victory and defeat, because if we lose one or both of them then we'll also have lost any chance of air cover for a landing operation in the islands. And such an operation is going to be difficult enough *with* air cover.' He paused again. 'Right, that is the why. Any questions there before we go on to the how?'

Jesus, Docherty thought. Was the Task Force that vulnerable? Apparently it was. In which case, the whole thing made sense and he had no questions.

'Right,' Strachan continued, 'the how. You will be flown to Ascension, and then flown on from there to the Task Force. A parachute drop, I'm afraid. You will receive the full briefing on the *Resource*, and it should be no more than a couple of days before you are flown in by helicopter. How long you remain will depend on the situation, but it should be no more than a fortnight – because by that time the bridgehead on the islands should be more than secure. Extraction will be by submarine, from a predetermined location at a set hour on a three-day pattern. Any questions?'

'Who are the other lucky bastards?' Razor asked.

Strachan looked at Weighell, who shrugged. 'I don't suppose there's any harm in your knowing. Assuming we can get them out of West Falkland in one piece, it'll be one of G Squadron's patrols: Major Brookes, plus Troopers Matthews, Laurel and Moseley.'

There were good-natured groans. 'And where are they going to find a helicopter large enough to carry us and Hedge?' Wacko wanted to know.

'If we're going in by helicopter, why can't we be taken out that way?' Docherty asked.

'It'll be a one-way trip going in,' Strachan admitted.

'So what happens to the crew?' Ben asked.

'That's still to be decided,' Weighell butted in. 'As is the question of uniform. How would you four feel about going in without uniforms, knowing there's a risk the Argentinians might treat you as spies?'

'I'll wear pyjamas,' Wacko said, 'if it gets us to do something other than sit around in England.'

'Why would we not be wearing uniforms?' Docherty asked. This was beginning to smell a little, he thought.

'Because the Government may want to disown you,' Weighell said bluntly. 'There's a lot of political ramifications to this, as you can guess. The Foreign Office is worried about losing friends if we look too aggressive . . .'

'Jesus Christ, boss, this is a *war*, isn't it?' Wacko wanted to know.

'To us it is,' Weighell said drily. 'The Foreign Office likes to think it's considering the long-term implications. Trade, that sort of thing . . .'

'Money,' Razor said disgustedly.

'Not just,' Weighell said. 'They have to keep our allies sweet, too, or the enemy will find it a lot easier to replace and upgrade its weaponry – particularly the Exocets.'

'The fucking French,' Razor said with feeling.

Great, Docherty was thinking. We put our lives on the line and the fucking Government is not prepared to even admit we're British soldiers. 'What are we supposed to be, if we get caught?' he asked. 'Albanians?'

'I don't know,' Weighell said, as honestly as he could.

'I guess the trick is not to get caught,' Ben offered.

'Right,' Wacko agreed.

Docherty looked at them. 'Razor?' he asked.

The Londoner shrugged. 'Let's worry about it when we have to. It sounds like an important job, boss,' he added quietly.

Docherty smiled inwardly. 'Aye, it does,' he agreed. And why the hell not, he told himself. He smiled at Weighell. 'Looks like we're your men, boss,' he said quietly.

'I thought you might be,' Weighell said.

'Your transport leaves for Brize Norton in a couple of hours,' Strachan added. 'I doubt if any of you have loved ones, but if you have you can use the Admin Office phone to give them the good news.' He stopped at the door. 'You lucky bastards,' he said affectionately, and disappeared.

Weighell wished them all good luck, then drew Docherty aside. 'Just wanted to make sure you know,' he said, 'that if the Government disowns you the Regiment won't.'

Docherty nodded. 'I'll tell the others,' he said.

When Weighell had gone the four of them stood there looking at each other. 'Just when I was getting used to the idea of a long and boring life,' Razor said. 'I'd better ring my mum.'

'I'm off home,' Wacko said. 'I'll be back in an hour.'

The other three trooped across to the Admin Office, and took turns using the phone and flirting with the secretaries. Razor woke his mum up, and spent ten minutes telling her not to worry. When he came off the phone there were tears in his eyes, which he tried unsuccessfully as far as Docherty was concerned, to conceal. Ben spoke to his mother as well, though it seemed as if she did all the talking.

Docherty spoke to one of his sisters, who said she would pick a good time to tell his mother. He then decided, on the spur of the moment, to ring Liam McCall, but the phone rang and rang until a woman he did not know answered. 'Tell Liam that Jamie rang,' Docherty told her. 'Tell him I've gone to feed the penguins and exorcize a few demons.'

4

Staring into fog was almost hypnotic, Hedge thought. Since the onset of daylight banks of the stuff had drifted up Falkland Sound, as if taking over the night's job of rendering the world less visible. And if the experience of the last few days was anything to go by, it would hang around until night came back on shift.

'Another busy day dawns,' he murmured to Mozza, who was taking his time retreating to bed. 'At least we can all have a decent meal.'

There were compensations for the grey-out. Each man could spend time conceiving and preparing his own gourmet feast from the dried menu available, and cook it up on the tiny hexamine stove each carried. It tasted good, it warmed him up, and the whole process consumed time which might otherwise have been given over to boredom. On clear days and nights, by contrast, the fare was all cold: biscuits, chocolate and cheese. Or, for variety, cheese, chocolate and biscuits. The preparation time was what it took to remove the wrappers.

'I'd like my steak medium to well done,' Hedge whispered after the retreating Mozza. 'With chips and mushrooms and a pint of red plonk.'

This reminded Hedge of his full bladder. Another

of the advantages of fog, he thought, as he relieved himself on the open hillside a few yards away from the OP, was an honest-to-goodness natural piss. On cold, clear mornings you had to do it inside the hide, and let it out in dribs and drabs to minimize the tell-tale plume of steam. If the Argies were watching they would think they were encircled by men with prostate problems.

Hot meals, flowing piss – you're really grasping at straws, he told himself, as he eased his bulk back into the hide and double-checked that the camouflage netting was correctly in place. Let's face it, Hedge, he reminded himself, everything you're wearing is wet and likely to remain so for the foreseeable future, your feet are either numb with cold or feel like they're sharing your socks with a pair of dead fish, and you've no idea how much longer you're going to be stuck in this God-forsaken hillside on this God-forsaken island in this God-forsaken ocean. Your boat home is probably being sunk even as you think, and your PC has probably just woken up with the idea of checking out the enemy minefields tonight under cover of fog. Is this what you joined the fucking SAS for?

It probably was.

After all, what else would he be doing? If he was not in the Army he would be either unemployed or bored out of his mind. Or in prison like two of his schoolfriends, both of whom had hated their working lives so much that they had lost any idea of self-control at the weekends. They had half-killed some poor Paki just because he gave them the wrong sort of smile.

Hedge sighed to himself. He had never liked Pakis much himself, but since being in the Army, and particularly since being in the SAS, his feelings had changed, at least a bit. He supposed being in close contact with the Gurkhas in Hong Kong had made him think about such things, but he had the feeling that the more important changes were in how he felt about himself. People picked on others when they were scared or feeling hard done by, he reckoned, and he felt pretty satisfied with the way his life was going. He might not like sitting in a cold puddle for days on end but he had no doubts about what he was there for. And in his experience that was something really worth knowing.

At least this fog would clear, he thought to himself, staring out at the giant shroud. He remembered an Incredible Hulk story in which the hero found himself trapped in a parallel universe that was contained in a speck of dust on someone's knee, and idly wondered whether he had been miniaturized and dropped into the head of a dinosaur's Q-tip.

They had been the only passengers on the coach from Stirling Lines to the RAF base at Brize Norton, and they proved to be the only human cargo carried south by the Hercules C-130 to Ascension.

'I begin to understand why Ascension hasn't been developed for tourism,' Docherty said nine hours later. The fuel tanks which had been added to increase the C-130's flight range made the aircraft even more cramped than before, and the web seats had lost none of their capacity to torture each and every limb.

'That and the fact that there's fuck-all there,' Razor agreed.

'What do you mean?' Wacko wanted to know, 'the place is full of history.'

'I don't think G Squadron's Wankathon counts as real history,' Razor said.

'Napoleon was exiled here, you ignorant bastard.'

'What, the Man from Uncle?' Ben asked deadpan.

'No, you moron, the French guy. Napoleon Bonaparte.'

'Is he still around?' Razor wanted to know.

Docherty smiled to himself and refrained from pointing out that Napoleon had been exiled to St Helena, 800 miles away. Sometimes the three of them seemed so different, but at others they had an uncanny knack for following the same thread of absurdity. And usually in the same depraved direction. Their mothers probably loved them.

'Napoleon had one thing on you,' Wacko was saying, 'he could show a bit of restraint. When was the last time you said "not tonight" to yourself? Or to a woman, even?'

'No, no,' Razor insisted, 'you've got it all wrong. When he said "not tonight, Josephine" he meant no *TV* tonight, because he wanted to get her straight to bed.'

'They didn't have TV then, you idiot.'

'Yes, you idiot, it was the radio,' Ben said. 'Josephine was an *Archers* addict.'

And so it went on for most of the remaining hour of the flight. It took up the time, it stopped Wacko thinking about Anne and Brendan, stopped Razor worrying about his mum, and pushed Morag's ultimatum to the back of Ben's mind. It stopped them all from thinking about their aching limbs or the war awaiting them.

At Ascension's Wideawake Airfield the four of them stepped almost buoyantly onto the tarmac and surveyed the surrounding scenery. It was only just after dawn, but already they could feel the heat building, and there was no shortage of activity across the airfield. Supplies and aircraft seemed to be competing for space, and the one long runway looked more like a corridor than the usual road set on a large lawn. In one direction the remains of the volcano which had created the island rose up behind the various buildings ringing the airfield; in the other a multitude of naval vessels were rolling in the blue Atlantic.

'That way, chums,' the pilot told them with an airy wave of the hand, and they eventually managed to locate a less than enthusiastic welcoming committee in one of the temporary offices. He was not expecting any more SAS men, had nowhere to put them, and thought they must be joking if they thought a plane would take them on south. 'The whole fuckin' Army's leaving tomorrow, and some of them are having to use rowing boats.'

'No wonder Napoleon died here,' Razor muttered.

The sergeant eyed them all fondly. 'Why don't you go and find some breakfast in the Volcano Club while I get your gear out of the plane and try and sort something out,' he suggested.

It was not a bad idea: the steaks were thick and juicy, the fried eggs all unbroken, the chips elegantly poised between too crisp and too greasy. After demolishing their plates all four of them laid themselves out for sleep on rows of chairs, and Wacko at least was soon snoring with enough gusto to frighten the Navy.

Docherty found himself unable to doze, and sat back up, gazing out of the wide windows at the

Vulcans, Nimrods and Starlifters strewn across the airfield. For a moment he thought he was in one of those old war films, and that at any moment they would be trooping out to their planes, revving propellers, trundling up into the sky. But this was real, he thought, looking around at his comatose companions. All this effort to put right what a few moronic generals probably thought up over breakfast one morning. What a farce.

But at least it was their own farce, Docherty thought. And he had no problem with the idea of using force to show that walking into other people's countries was beyond the pale. It was just that somehow this all seemed a bit like overkill, and it worried him a little. Not a lot, but a little. Which was still too much.

Docherty had always thought the phrase 'yours not to reason why' was one of the dumbest things a soldier could ever tell himself. It made a lot more sense to spend some time working out why, because then it became a hell of lot easier 'to do or die'.

On Friday 7 May the day dawned on the hillside above Port Howard without any accompanying fog. There seemed to be a pattern, Brookes thought – one day with, one day without. He could think of no conceivable reason why this should be so, but then he did not understand how flicking a switch could fill a room with light either. Science was for the scientists to deal with.

It was by no means as bright as the day before yesterday had been, but he could see all he needed to of the settlement and camp below. Not much had happened since the visit of the inspection team – if that was what they were – two days previously. That day there had been a lot of standing in line, a lot of polishing weapons, a lot of salutes. In the hour before dusk there had even been a football tournament, with four teams playing three games on a sloping pitch beyond the camp. Brookes's knowledge of football was almost non-existent, but according to Stanley the level of technique had been high.

Which was hardly the sort of information the Task Force needed. Nor did Brookes feel that Stanley's masterplan – 'Let's go down and steal their ball' – would inspire much support in the ladies' toilet aboard the *Resource*.

The information they did need had mostly been gathered, and transmitted in code by short burst on the patrol's Clansman the previous night. It would have been a miracle if the Argentinians' Direction Finding (DF) equipment had picked up the transmission, let alone pinpointed its source, and as yet there were no signs in the camp below of any patrol activity.

Mozza's original guess-timate of the enemy's strength had been almost spot-on. There were between 920 and 950 men in the camp below, constituting, if the flag flying rather foolishly from one building had any validity, the 5th Regiment of the 3rd Brigade. The men were well armed, with rifles and SMGs comparable, if not superior, to those carried by the British, and they were energetically adding new trench positions and minefields around the settlement to those already dug out and laid.

A gun emplacement had appeared during the previous day's fog, complete with a 105mm artillery piece now pointing out into the Sound. It had presumably been stored in one of the outhouses, most likely with the aim of concealing it from satellite or other high-altitude surveillance. Now, with the prospect of a British landing drawing nearer, it was being made ready. Brookes thought that probably meant there were no others hidden away, but at some point he would have to decide whether the element of doubt necessitated a closer look.

He watched through the telescope as one of the enemy soldiers emerged from one of the sheds with a bucket and tipped what looked like vegetable peelings onto a growing pile. There was no doubt that their camp was growing dirtier and more untidy by the day, a fact which Brookes considered highly significant. On paper the Argentinians were numerous and well armed, but this unit at least was lacking in the sort of self-discipline which made for an efficient fighting force.

It was hard to put his finger on it exactly, but there was a general sloppiness about it all. They did not want to be here, that much was clear. Smiles were few and far between, scowls worn almost as part of the badly-kept uniforms. And the ordinary soldiers seemed incredibly young; hardly beyond the pimple stage. That was it, Brookes suddenly realized: this was an adolescent army, which might prove long on courage but would almost certainly prove woefully short on concentrated or prolonged effort.

This was one of two fatal weaknesses in the Argentinians' position. The other was the troops' lack of mobility. Maybe the enemy had 100 helicopters ready to transport this regiment to where it might be needed, but Brookes very much doubted it. When the Marines came ashore in a couple of weeks time, across the Sound 20 miles or so to the north and east, these troops would simply be stuck here in Port Howard, 1000 helpless and probably thankful spectators.

Brookes was smiling to himself at this prospect as he noticed the patrol leaving the camp below, obviously headed up into the hills. He watched for some fifteen minutes as the line of twenty-two men, sometimes visible, sometimes not, steadily climbed an invisible track which would take them a quarter of a mile or so to the east of the hide.

Then their line of march veered towards him.

He woke Hedge, and told the big man to wake Stanley and Mozza. When they were all assembled – as much as any four men could 'assemble' in a cross-shaped hide only 30 inches deep – he told them why they had been woken. 'There's an Argie patrol headed this way,' he said softly. 'Twenty-one of them. In another couple of minutes we'll have to go over to hand-signals, so . . .' He took a deep breath. 'It's just gone three o'clock,' he went on, 'so there's only about two more hours of light. If they spot the hide I'm for taking them on. With any luck we can get ourselves back over the ridge, and it'll be dark before they manage to get any reinforcements up here. What do you think?' he asked, in the democratic way the SAS took for granted.

'Sounds good to me, boss,' Hedge answered.

'Piece of cake,' Stanley agreed.

'What should we try and take with us?' Mozza asked, and wondered why his voice sounded so calm when the rest of him suddenly seemed anything but.

'The MP5s, the M203,' Brookes said. 'And we'll need the radio, of course. Sorry, Mozza, but you will have to take the extra weight. Get everything else out of your bergen now.' He turned back to the outside world. The enemy patrol was only about a quarter of a mile away, and seemed to be both spreading out and headed in their direction.

'We won't leave you behind,' Stanley was reassuring Mozza. 'We can't do without the radio.'

'He's young and fit,' Hedge observed. 'He hasn't spoiled himself with self-indulgence like some I could mention.'

'No more talk,' Brookes said curtly. 'Hand-signals only. If I yell then we're up and at 'em.'

The next ten minutes seemed more like ten hours, particularly to the three men who could see nothing, who could do nothing but wait and wonder and try to be ready when the time came. For Brookes the time may have gone faster, but at an even greater cost to his nerves. The Argentinian soldiers, each carrying an automatic rifle, were obviously intent on combing this particular hillside, though whether as part of a random sweep or because someone thought he had seen something suspicious Brookes had no idea. At any rate they were advancing across the slope in a long, sweeping line, each soldier walking a parallel path some 20 yards from his nearest compatriot.

Such a wide gap, Brookes reckoned, increased their chance of going undetected. But it also meant that if the hide was spotted, there was next to no chance of their killing many of the enemy, or of getting away.

The line drew slowly nearer. Brookes could see the face of the nearest soldier, a boy of not much more than seventeen, and prayed he had bad eyesight. On his present path he would come within a few feet of the hide, and could hardly fail to notice something. He was now about 50 yards away.

Brookes signalled '50' to the others in the hide.

They sat there stony-faced, wondering how their own breathing could sound so loud. Hedge felt his stomach silently rumble, and prayed that they would not be betrayed by one of his farts. Mozza was fighting a mad desire to shout out something, anything, to break the overwhelming silence.

The sound of boots swishing through wet grass grew louder. The boy was almost on top of them when his next in line further up the hill said something in Spanish, something about someone called Pérez which Brookes could not quite make out. It hardly mattered though, for whatever it was it made the boy laugh and look away at just the moment when a downward glance to his left might well have killed himself and all four men in the hide.

The swish of the boots began to fade, replaced by the sound of four Englishmen exhaling with relief. More minutes passed, rather less traumatically, until Brookes was able to report in a soft voice that the enemy patrol had passed out of sight around the far shoulder of the hill.

'I reckon this hide should get a perfect score for technical merit,' Stanley said proudly.

'Either that or the Argies were looking for a restaurant,' Hedge agreed.

Brookes thought he would tell them about the fortunate joke at some later date, preferably after the war was over.

On Ascension Island Docherty's patrol had eventually been found four empty bunks in a disused school, and nine hours' sleep had done wonders for their individual states of mind. They had then done exercises and gone for a much-interrupted run: on Ascension, it seemed, everyone was busy building personal empires and putting up fences around them. In the meantime the Falklands landing force was preparing for its departure the following day, and the small supply boats whizzed to and fro between the larger ships and shore as the fork-lift trucks drew patterns on the airfield tarmac.

The opportunities for entertainment were rather more limited. As Razor noted, the Navy boys could climb into their bunks together, but for real soldiers there was only the Volcano Club. Which was not saying much, Docherty thought to himself after the second pint. He was taking it more slowly than usual, aware that his body was still recovering from the previous weeks' abuse. The other three seemed to be taking their cue from him, or maybe they too were hyper-conscious of how important it was, in view of what lay ahead, not to risk their level of fitness.

The same could not be said for most of the other revellers. One group, on the far side of the room, seemed to be drinking like there was no tomorrow, and making enough noise to drown out the conversations of the remaining clientele. Every now and then they would burst into a new verse set to the melody of 'Summer Holiday': the most recent of which had featured the immortal line 'napalm sticks to spics'.

'Arseholes,' Razor muttered to no one in particular.

'They're just REMFs,' Ben said. 'Rear-echelon mother-fuckers,' he enunciated carefully. 'And you can bet your life they've never seen what napalm can do up close.'

'It's one of those things,' Docherty said. 'It's always the ones who know nothing who make all the fucking noise.' He had a strong desire to go over and make his feelings felt.

'It's like racism,' Wacko said. 'The places it's strongest in England are the places where there aren't any blacks. Like East Anglia.'

Razor glanced across at him, surprised. He had never exactly thought of Wacko as a racist, but the man was hardly famous for his liberal opinions. Then the connection hit him. With a foreign father, Wacko would have learnt the hard way.

The singing swelled once more. 'We won't cry for you Argentina, we'll just send you our Polaris . . .'

The four of them were saved by an Air Force officer, who told them that they would be leaving at 0700 hours the next morning. Suddenly all the noise and ugly jingoism seemed beside the point. Unlike the singers they were on their way to war.

They were in the helicopter: Francisco, herself and the two security men. Francisco was on the floor, smiling up at her, despite the wires which held his wrists and ankles in a knot behind his arched back, despite the burns and bruises visible on his face, despite the six bricks cemented together and attached by chains to the tangle of wires.

'Please, no,' she implored the security men. 'I'll do anything if you'll let him go.'

The one with the thin moustache smirked at her. 'You'll do anything anyway,' he said.

'She already has,' his partner said. 'Everyone at the School had her – she was such a nice piece of ass when she first arrived. And she was really eager to please.'

'No, no, that's not true,' she told Francisco desperately, and he seemed to believe her. His smile never wavered, even when they pulled him across the floor, said 'adiós, pig', and pushed the block of bricks out into space. Then an expression of surprise seemed to suffuse his face, and he looked up once at her as his fingers grasped at the doorframe, before the foot smashed into his face and he was gone.

And then the face was slowly drifting down through the water, his hair waving, the smile fading into an open mouth, exhaling bubbles . . .

She woke with a start, shaking like a leaf. The church bells of Rio Gallegos were ringing for morning Mass.

If only Sharon could see him now, Stanley thought to himself. He was walking some five yards behind Brookes, closer when the mist thickened, further apart when it thinned. Generally though it seemed to be growing thicker the closer they got to Port Howard and sea level.

The previous night the patrol had received a coded radio message from the SAS operations centre on the *Resource*. They were being pulled out on the following night. No explanation was given, merely the coordinates of the pick-up zone some five miles away and their helicopter taxi's ETA.

It was hard to feel too sad about leaving their waterlogged home on a windy slope, but for Brookes the horrible suspicion arose that this might prove his last-ever mission for the SAS. If it had to be, then it had to be, but if so then it was going to be damn-near perfect. There was still one large gap in their knowledge which they needed to fill: the nature of whatever it was that the Argies had stored in the two large corrugated sheds close by the jetty on the inlet. They were probably full of corned beef or toilet paper or pictures of General Galtieri, but there was always the chance they might contain something posing more of a threat to the upcoming British landing. Surface-to-air missiles, for example.

There was only one way to find out, he had said, and that was to go and take a look. The others had agreed in principle, but disputed Brookes's proposed timing. He had intended to do the traditional thing, and go at once, under the cover of darkness. Stanley had disagreed, arguing that the early-morning fog would be just as concealing, and that the Argentinians would be unlikely to be using any thermal-imaging capacity they possessed at such an hour. The trooper's argument had convinced Brookes, which was why the two of them were now nearing a camp of 1000 enemy soldiers protected by little more than a curtain of water droplets and two silenced Heckler & Koch MP5 sub-machine-guns.

There was the sudden sound of laughter ahead and to their right, and Stanley noticed the hairs on his wrist were standing up on end.

Ahead of him he saw Brookes move his extended right arm slowly down and up, and accordingly slowed down. Then the PC moved his arm again, this time from the diagonal to the vertical, signalling a renewed advance.

What fun, Stanley told himself.

Brookes veered off to the left, as certain as he could be that the two of them were inside the protective ring of minefields. According to his map of the settlement, first drawn from sight and then transferred to memory, a house should soon be looming out of the fog slightly to their right.

112

A few more yards and it did. Brookes congratulated himself and signalled Stanley forward to join him. At that moment a loud voice echoed in the silence: 'Tea's made, Ted.'

It was almost shocking in both its ordinariness and its Englishness. The temptation to wander across and partake of a cup was almost overwhelming. Brookes and Stanley stared at each other, and both broke into the same stupid grin, white teeth gleaming in their blackened faces.

Brookes led off again, skirting what looked like rotting string beans on a line of canes and climbing over a low hedge and into a muddy lane. The simultaneous sound of feet and murmured Spanish sent him back the way he had come, and the two of them crouched down behind the foliage, MP5s at the ready.

Two uniformed figures slowly materialized out of the mist, carrying what looked like a packing case of ammunition. It was obviously heavy enough to absorb all their attention, because they passed by breathing heavily and dematerialized once more. Brookes and Stanley would have had no trouble coming up behind them and slitting each throat from ear to ear, but it had been agreed that this particular walk on the wild side should remain unknown to the enemy if at all possible. There was, after all, little chance of them slitting 1000 throats on the one trip.

They stood motionless for another minute, ears straining for sounds of any other activity. All they could hear was the murmur of voices way behind them, and the occasional squawk of a seabird somewhere out in front.

They resumed their progress, following the muddy

lane in what Brookes assumed was the direction of the
jetty. The sound of water lapping against the wooden
piers confirmed as much. The dark shape of the first
corrugated warehouse loomed out of the mist.

The two men inched along the side wall, and
Brookes put an eye round the corner. There was
no one in sight, but that was hardly surprising
when visibility was less than 10 yards. He signalled
Stanley to follow and started edging his way along
the front.

The main doors were shut, but the large, rusty
padlock – 'Made in Warrington' – had not been fastened. More sloppiness, Brookes thought to himself.
He listened up against the door, and heard no sounds
coming from inside. Signalling Stanley to cover him,
he pulled the sliding door to the left as silently as
he could.

Inside there was hardly any light, and it took their
eyes several seconds to adjust to the gloom. When
they did it was to an unexpected sight. The shed was
empty save for two tables and about twenty blank
road signs. Only one seemed to have been completed:
it stood proudly against the far wall, reading 'BAHIA
ZORRO 57 KILOMETROS'.

'Fox Bay,' Brookes translated for Stanley, and the
two men looked at each other with disbelieving faces.
The enemy was concentrating on getting the islands'
road signs right! There were not even any *roads*
worthy of the name. Brookes wondered what they
would discover in the other shed – copies of *Teach
Yourself Spanish For Sheep*?

It turned out to be empty, save for some shearing
equipment. The Argentinian garrison at Port Howard
was what it had seemed from the hide: a concentration

of force entirely lacking in mobility; no threat to anyone other than the dozen or so locals. And even the latter seemed to be still enjoying their breakfast cup of tea.

Brookes led off once more, back the way they had come. It might not be the safest route when it came to unexpected meetings with the enemy, but many hours of telescopic observation had seemed to indicate it was free of mines. And the fog, if anything, seemed to be thickening.

They passed down the lane, passed by the house where they had heard the English voices, and started up the hill away from the settlement. They were just passing the familiar landmark of an abandoned oil barrel when the shadows came out of the fog.

The three enemy soldiers saw Brookes at the same moment he saw them, but training and speed of reaction made all the difference. They were on their way back into base, not expecting trouble, their minds on breakfast or a warm bed. Two were carrying their automatic rifles by the barrel, one had his over the shoulder, and Brookes's cradled MP5 had killed the first two while they were still juggling. The third actually tripped in his shock, causing Brookes's second burst to miss him, but it seemed that Stanley, stepping swiftly out from behind the PC, had prevented the man from getting his finger to the trigger with an accurate burst through his chest.

Then, almost posthumously it seemed, the rifle fired once as the man crumpled, shattering the silence.

'Shit,' Brookes said with feeling. He thought for a second, half his mind listening for an alarm in the camp behind him. It came as a slowly swelling chorus of questioning voices and sporadic shouts.

'Let's at least get them off the track,' he whispered.

They lugged two of the men – boys, really, judging from their faces – some 10 yards into the fog, praying as they did so that they were not trespassing on a minefield. Stanley then dragged the third to join his comrades while Brookes waited on the track, listening to what sounded like a headless chickens' convention in the camp below.

'Let's make some speed,' he told the returning Stanley, and the two of them started up the hill at a half-run, the voices growing ever fainter behind them. For the moment they were safe, but only for the moment. To make matters worse, Brookes had the distinct impression that the fog was beginning to thin. If it evaporated entirely, he did not think much of their chances of escaping detection. Looking for a possible hide was one thing; looking for one you knew was there was another matter entirely. And with three of their comrades dead the Argentinians would hardly need motivating.

When he and Stanley got back to the hide, Brookes knew, there would have to be some swift decisions. He tried to get his own thoughts in order as Stanley navigated their way through the fog.

It took them an hour to reach 'home', where Hedge and Mozza were relieved to see them. They had spent the same hour nervously waiting to find out why the enemy had fired a shot, and whether he had hit anything valuable, like Brookes or Stanley.

'Decision time, lads,' Brookes insisted. He looked at his watch. 'We have sixteen and a half hours before the pick-up, at least seven of them in daylight. We can either head out now or stay put until dark. If we go,

116

we risk being caught in the open if the fog clears. If we stay, we risk being found or so hemmed in that we can't make the pick-up at all.'

'Nice choice,' Stanley murmured.

'Isn't it? Preferences, gentlemen?'

'Yes,' Hedge offered. 'I'd feel better on the move. If the Argies don't find us during the day then they'll be out in strength tonight, and we were warned that they probably have thermal imagers. At least while the fog stays put their choppers can't fly, and we'll have no problem keeping ahead of the foot soldiers.'

'OK. Mozza?'

'Sounds right to me.' The thought of another long and tense vigil, cramped in the sopping hide, with no real chance of fighting their way out if they were discovered, held no appeal at all.

'Stanley?'

'Suits me. Though I'd feel happier if we had a couple of those hand-held surface-to-air missiles "Air Troop" got their grubby paws on.'

'I'd feel happier if we could find a greasy spoon,' Hedge said. 'Eggs, bacon, beans, sausage, mushroom, burger, onions and a double portion of chips. All of it hot.'

Brookes licked his lips despite himself. His wife was always going on about his cholesterol level. 'Let's get packed and out of here,' he said, 'before the Argies have us for breakfast.'

A little under ten minutes later they were ready to move. Stanley led the way, the others following in the accustomed order, though considerably closer together than usual because of the poor visibility. The hide's camouflage had been left in slight disarray, on the off-chance that the Argentinians would not only spot it, but waste valuable pursuit time by laying siege to an empty hole in the ground.

Since the most counter-productive thing they could do now was to get lost, the patrol's progress was slow, with Brookes and Stanley checking and double-checking each change of direction against their illuminated compasses and what little they could see of the terrain. Generally they were climbing, but the grain of the land ran against their chosen direction, so it was often a case of two steps upward, one step down. The only apparent witnesses to their march were sheep, most of whom expressed their resentment at the intrusion with a succession of indignant bleats.

All four soldiers continually examined the fog for signs of thinning, and were frequently convinced that they could detect as much. But the overall level of visibility somehow remained as restricted as ever. At around three they gathered beneath the lip of a convenient ridge for a ten-minute rest and a silent lunch of chocolates, biscuits and three-day-old rainwater. Mozza, looking around at the other three and the cocoon of mist they inhabited, found himself thinking about *Dr Who*, the favourite TV series of his childhood. The reason, he realized, was that the foreshortened horizon made it look like they were in a studio.

They strapped their bergens back on and resumed their march. Once more it seemed obvious that the fog was thinning. And this time it really was: slowly, but definitely.

After climbing up a small valley and crossing another ridge line, Brookes called a halt. Visibility was now about 100 yards and increasing rapidly. Somehow ahead of them to the west a pale wash of sunlight was trying to make itself seen.

'Scrapes,' Brookes said. The others groaned, but nevertheless took to the job with all the speed they could muster. The turf was carefully removed, the four shallow trenches dug, the excavated earth stuffed under a convenient slab of overhanging rock, and the hessian nets fixed for relaying the turf roofs. Less than fifteen minutes after Brookes's order the four of them were each lying on damp soil in relative darkness, listening to their own hearts beating.

It was hardly a moment too soon. Their last view of the outside world had been of mist peeling away from the land and rising into the sky in great swathes, like the smoke of gunfire escaping from a nineteenth-century battlefield. Now, through the gaps afforded by the clump of tussock grass above his head, Brookes could see patches of blue sky. What a life, he thought. He sincerely hoped any future wars the SAS got involved in offered a better climate and more amenable terrain.

'Action stations!' the RAF dispatcher shouted above the C-130 engines. 'Get your gear ready, lads!' He waved an imaginary wand, and the plane's tailgate started lowering itself, letting in the world with a roar and rush.

The four men began the tricky manœuvres necessary for inserting themselves in divers' dry suits. It would have been hard enough in the middle of the pitch at Parkhead, Docherty thought, let alone in this space between supply cases where there was barely room to swing a cat. But eventually they were all suitably encased, and zipping each other up like happy debutantes. Fins were stuffed into belts, and then each man hoisted himself into the parachute harness which had been adjusted to his measurements before their take-off from Ascension. Once the distress flares had been strapped to their wrists they could start worrying in earnest.

His three comrades were not especially nervous about jumping, but Razor had never taken to it. He knew his fears were no more sensible than those of anyone getting on a plane, but somehow the knowledge did not help. When all was said and done, the ground was a bloody long way down and bloody hard to boot. It was all very well them saying the odds of both parachutes failing were a million to one. If odds like that never came up then no one would do the football pools, would they? And as for jumping into the ocean: well, it might look all soft and welcoming but that water down there was hard as concrete if you hit it from this height. And even if it all went well those idiots in the Navy still had to find you before your balls froze and dropped off.

Look on the bright side, Razor told himself, at least there were no sharks. Or at least he hoped not. Jesus, what had brought that thought into his head? A picture of Corinna's face crossed his mind, and he visualized her up the ladder in the restaurant, painting the ceiling, the overalls tight around her bum. Now that was the type of thought he needed for a leap into oblivion.

'Five minutes,' the dispatcher in charge yelled at them. The pallets holding all their gear were already waiting on the tailgate ramp, and when the cargo-hold light turned green the team of dispatchers, all wearing full parachute gear in case of accidents, started rolling them off the end and out into space.

They were next. Docherty took the lead position,

knowing that most jumpers, no matter how experienced, still found that first look down a touch unnerving. He rather enjoyed it. Inverted vertigo, he thought to himself, looking down at the churning grey sea 1000 feet below. The only ships he could see were way to either side, but at that moment one slid almost directly beneath them. The pallets containing their bergens, weaponry, signalling equipment and personal kit were floating down gracefully.

The dispatcher slapped him on the back, and he launched himself out into the C-130's slipstream, into the first sensation of being hammered forward, then the relief of the harness tugging at the body, the open canopy filling the sky. The thought crossed his mind that it was like going down a slide as a kid: the series of familiar physical sensations, the excitement.

He jettisoned the reserve chute, pulled down on both steering toggles to reduce his forward motion and unclipped the reserve hooks from the main parachute as the ocean rushed up to meet him. A split second before impact he hit the harness release, eliminating the risk of drag and allowing the canopy to go with the wind.

The water was cold, even through the dry suit, but he felt exhilarated, as he always did after a jump. He managed to get the fins on, inflated his life-jacket, and trod water as he tried to get his head high enough for a look around. He could see nothing but waves for a moment, then one of the others became suddenly visible. Half a mile or so beyond the bobbing head a frigate was sailing blithely by across his line of sight.

How long could a man survive in water this cold, Docherty wondered. It would be rather an ironic end to his career – being transported halfway round the world just to be dropped from a great height into a watery grave. 'Where are you, you bastards,' he murmured to himself.

As if on cue, a rigid raider suddenly appeared not 20 yards away, headed his way. A hand reached down with a knife to puncture the life-jacket and make it easier to pull him aboard. Razor was already sitting there, a huge smile of relief on his face.

In his scrape Mozza was composing a letter to Lynsey, even though he knew he would forget most of it before he had the chance to write anything down. She would be worried, he guessed, and so he would not be telling her much of the truth – always assuming he would be allowed to. Nobody had said anything, but he supposed there would be some sort of restrictions.

He had not seen any penguins yet, so there was nothing much to report to three-year-old Hannah. When it came down to it he supposed the only thing he really wanted to say was that he loved them both and missed them. For a moment he had a picture in his head of Lynsey's face a few inches from his own in her candlelit bedroom and he almost felt choked with yearning.

A few feet away Hedge was not missing anyone half as much as a good meal. It was his only real grudge against the SAS: the way the bosses delighted in putting such a distance between the men and any half-decent canteen. There should be an SAS equivalent of meals-on-wheels, he decided, delivering hot meals to the various OPs. Either that or the Navy could run a take-away pizza service from one of the carriers. The OPs could order by radio.

He started working out the Morse code for extra pepperoni.

Stanley, for once, was not thinking about sex, Sharon, or sex with Sharon. Well, not directly, anyway. He was remembering the ten-point guide to the ideal woman which he and Barry Saunders had made up one night, sitting in a car outside the Divis Flats. It had been a good way to spend a few hours, but it all seemed a bit stupid now. Fuck knew why. His needs had not changed, or at least he hoped not. It was bloody Mozza's fault, Stanley thought, with all that crap about love and understanding and equality. Women were not equal, no matter which way you looked at it. If they were they would have them in the SAS, right?

OK, so that was crap reasoning, Stanley told himself ruefully. But the point was . . .

The drone of the helicopter forced its way into his consciousness. Number one – great breasts with great nipples, he silently mouthed as the drone grew louder. Number two – legs long enough for skiing on. It seemed almost on top of them now. Number three – a kiss you could splash around in. It was on top of them, a black shape against the sky, and the down-draught from its blades was tugging at the knot of grass which covered the head end of his scrape.

But had it seen them? There was no way of knowing.

Suddenly the grass was swept away, leaving Stanley looking straight up at the belly of a Puma helicopter. He reached for the M16, and at almost the same moment a pilot's face appeared round the edge of the machine, staring straight down at him.

123

The head jerked back, the helicopter reared up and to one side, and Stanley realized there was no longer any risk of bringing it down on top of them — all in less than a second. He threw himself out of the scrape, brought the rifle with its grenade-launcher attachment to his shoulder, aimed at the open cockpit door and fired.

With a dramatic whoosh the grenade exploded inside the cockpit, catapulting one pilot out and instantly killing the other. The chopper itself fell like a stone, bounced once on the ridge and toppled over and out of sight, before a loud explosion and a sharp plume of smoke announced its total demise.

The four SAS men climbed to the top of the ridge, and looked down at the burning wreckage below. 'Nice shot, Stanley,' Brookes said over his shoulder, as he walked back down to examine the pilot who had been blown clear. He was decidedly dead.

Brookes rejoined the others. 'There's another hour or so of light,' he said. 'I don't think either of them had time to radio in, but we'd better get moving.'

They resumed the march, and spent that hour of light waiting for the tell-tale sound of distant rotor blades. But none came, and a further two-hour journey in the dark brought them to the flat valley earmarked as the pick-up zone. They slept and watched in two-hour shifts until near the designated time, then set out the infrared lights to guide their taxi in.

It arrived on time, the pilot in his PNGs looking like a refugee from *Star Trek*. 'All aboard, chums,' he announced in a cheery whisper, 'and try not to dirty the seat-covers.'

Brookes asked how many of the other groups were being collected that night.

'Just you lot,' the pilot told him. 'Either you've been very naughty, or they've thought of somewhere worse to send you.'

5

At almost 23,000 tons the Royal Fleet Auxiliary *Resource* was one of the Task Force's larger ships. Surveying it from the helicopter which had brought them across from the *Hermes*, Docherty's patrol had expected a stateroom each, generous deck space for sunbathing and a personalized leisure centre. They had been given four bunks in the middle of a smoke-filled hold, and had needed to fight their way through G Squadron's clothes, equipment and bodies to stake even this claim.

They had swiftly been spotted.

'Oh, they're really scraping the barrel now,' someone observed. ''B' Squadron's arrived.'

'Looks like they've fallen overboard once already,' another voice noted.

Brookes's patrol returned to the *Resource* in the middle of the following night, but an unusually beneficent Navy found more amenable quarters for their first night back than the bunks in the hold. After glorious hot showers, they laid themselves out luxuriously on soft mattresses and dry sheets, and all but Brookes slept for ten hours straight. Even he managed nine.

They were allowed a copious brunch before business, and Hedge redeemed all the promises he had made himself over the past week. After draining a second huge mug of tea he leaned back in his seat, belched his satisfaction and wondered out loud: 'What now?'

'We'll soon know,' Brookes said. 'I don't suppose they pulled us out to send us home.' At least he hoped not. He looked at his watch. 'Come on, it's time we moved. Mustn't keep the Green Slime waiting.'

Several corridors, ladders and hatchways later the four of them were rapping on the door of the ship's ladies' toilet and being bidden to enter. Things had improved since their last visit. The tables in the centre were overlain with files, tide charts and military reference books, a mass of radio equipment was neatly stacked on benches, and maps were pinned to the cubicle doors. In one open cubicle doorway a hot-drinks machine was humming quietly to itself. Through the two portholes the grey-green sea was seething.

The Green Slime – as SAS Intelligence was (sometimes) affectionately known – was represented by Major Bill Hemmings, a tangle-haired Welshman whom Brookes had known in Oman. They were about the same age, but intelligence work was taking its toll on Hemmings, adding a few inches to his waistline and the first glimmerings of a second chin. His brain, though, showed no signs of going to seed.

After almost an hour had been consumed in debriefing their completed mission on West Falkland, he told them to help themselves to drinks from the machine and disappeared.

'He's gone for our medals,' Stanley observed.

'He's gone for a crap,' Hedge said.

Mozza stared out at the sea while Brookes scanned

the littered tables for any clues to their next mission. He found none.

Hemmings returned, trailing in his wake Docherty, Razor, Wacko and Ben. Some introductions were not necessary: Docherty and Brookes, though hardly friends, had often served in the same operations together, while Razor and Stanley knew each from the regimental football team. Everyone knew Hedge.

'You gentlemen,' Hemmings told them once everyone was seated, 'are Operation Backyard. Now since only half of you have any idea what this is all about, I'd better fill you in.'

After he had finished he asked if there were any questions. Brookes was feeling almost too happy for rational thought: this was indeed a mission worthy of ending one's active career – he could have hardly have asked for anything better. The other members of his patrol were still busy absorbing the idea when Docherty raised his voice.

'I have a couple,' he said. 'At Hereford we were told there were still two issues outstanding – the helicopter crew and the business of uniform. Has anything been decided?'

'On the former, yes. The Navy have found us some heroes, gentlemen . . .'

There were groans of disbelief, and murmurs of 'Kiss me, Hardy.'

Hemmings smiled sweetly at them. 'Who have volunteered – *volunteered*, gentlemen – to drop you lads off in Argentina, get as far into Chile as they can with what fuel they have left, and then bring the chopper down somewhere uninhabited and hide out for at least a week before giving themselves up. They could hardly do more, now, could they?'

There were groans of grudging acceptance.

'As for the uniforms, we're still waiting for the politicos to make up their minds.'

Docherty nodded. He did not mind what happened to him, but he wanted to be damn sure the younger ones knew what they were getting into before he agreed to lead them onto the mainland.

Isabel kept the Renault at 60kph as she drove it down the dead-straight section of the road from the Chilean border, and only occasionally bothered to check the rear mirror. Her mind told her each trip had to be more dangerous than the last, but her heart told her the threat was minimal. The local military was busy with the war, and the police in this part of the world were only accustomed to the problems posed by drunken oil workers. The security apparatus's natural habitat was in the cities of the north, and in any case the threat to the ruling class's security had always come from the people they exploited, not the agents of foreign powers.

They had been well prepared to catch her as a revolutionary, Isabel thought, but were ill equipped to catch her as a foreign spy. The thought brought a bitter smile to her lips.

That morning she had awoken with the word 'traitor' echoing in her brain, and no matter how vehemently she denied the charge to herself, the word refused to go away. 'So what?' she said out loud in English, the way Michael used to say it. The way he no doubt still did, she reminded herself. Somehow it was hard to think of him as still alive. Francisco seemed more alive, and he was dead.

She was a traitor to her country, but only insofar as

her country could be identified with the Junta and its retinue – the rich families, the bought union bosses, the animals who did the dirty work for all of them. She was no traitor to her class, nor to humanity as a whole.

But she was a traitor to Raul. That was the problem. That was what was beginning to get to her. He had done nothing to her, nothing to humanity. He had joined the Air Force because he loved to fly, and because it was a career that offered good money and social prestige. And maybe because, like most young men, he liked his girl to admire him in his uniform.

There were nothing wrong with such ambitions, or such a life. And because he had pursued them the Junta was sending him out to die against superior forces, and she was milking him of information under the guise of friendship, and then sending it to the enemy, increasing the chances of his being blown out of the sky.

In the plastic bag she had left under the stone there had been a full report on morale at the Rio Gallegos airbase, information on the number of nightly flights to Port Stanley, and Raul's considered opinions of both his fellow pilots and the defensive tactics employed by the British ships. Thanks to Raul's male-obsessive interest in numbers and lists – what Michael had always called the 'trainspotter mentality' – there was also a complete breakdown of the planes stationed at Rio Gallegos.

If this little information package did not get him killed, she thought savagely, then nothing would.

But the die was cast, at least for her. Guilt over Raul might be consuming the last of her soul, but the reasons for doing what she was doing seemed stronger with each week back in her native land. Argentina was like a nation in thrall, a country under a spell. Reason, judgement, any sense of real collective interest – all had been jettisoned in this fit of chauvinistic madness. Something or someone had to puncture this bubble, break the evil spell, and from where she stood it could only be the British. To help them was to help her country, and all the Rauls would have to pay the price.

Hemmings had told them that 'Backyard' would probably be set in motion on the night of either Thursday 13 May or the following Friday. Docherty's patrol was eager to get moving, but realized that Brookes and the other three needed several days to make a full recovery from their week on West Falkland. Any longer, though, and there was a danger Hedge would completely strip the *Resource* of edible food.

There was in any case quite a lot to do, particularly for the two PCs. They were responsible for deciding on, acquiring and checking the equipment each patrol would need. All eight of them were expected to familiarize themselves with all the available knowledge concerning the terrain, and be able to recognize any item of Argentinian military equipment from, as Hemmings put it, an Exocet to a standard-issue General's jockstrap.

'Sky blue and white, right?' Razor said with a grin.

'On the button, son,' Hemmings replied. 'Now go and study these diagrams.'

'They're not of Gabriella Sabatini, are they?' Stanley wanted to know.

When they were not memorizing aircraft silhouettes, Argentinian rank insignia and inadequate maps, the eight of them were getting used to operating two new state-of-the-art PRC 319 radios. These could be used for normal voice, burst Morse or liquid-crystal keyboard transmission via satellite. They were, as their proud instructor pointed out, Direction Finder Unfriendly.

As the two signalling specialists, Wacko and Mozza took the keenest interest in this new technology, but all eight of them were expected to be familiar with its operation.

Many of their non-study hours were devoted to strenuous physical exercises, as each man sought to reach and maintain the level of physical fitness they all knew they would need in the days to come.

The remaining hours were spent in sleeping, eating, noisy games of Cheat and various solitary pursuits. Each man wrote home, albeit with varying degrees of willingness and sincerity. Brookes and Wacko wrote letters to their wives that said nothing of what was in their hearts, while Mozza found it impossible to write about anything else. Docherty tried writing to Liam McCall about what he was feeling, and found he did not really know.

By Wednesday all of them were eager to go, and hoping that the earlier date had been chosen. But Brookes, delegated to extract the latest news from Hemmings, found the Green Slime man more than a touch reticent on the subject. The early date was extremely unlikely, Brookes was told, but beyond that Hemmings could not say. He was waiting for clearance from Northwood, and preferred not to speculate on why it had not yet arrived.

Brookes reported this back to the others, and Stanley, reaching deep into his vocabulary, expressed what they were all thinking: 'Fucking politicians couldn't run a fucking war if their fucking lives fucking depended on it.'

Bryan Weighell turned off the TV in the middle of the weather forecast. He was more interested in conditions in the South Atlantic than Britain, he thought. Desk work for the SAS was like life after death: your soul was still out there where the action was but your body was rotting by a telephone.

He had just watched pictures of the QE2's departure from Southampton that morning, with 5th Brigade lining the decks, and probably the bars as well. The diplomats were still shuttling to and fro like pompous penguins, but as far as he could see the die was cast, and a forced landing on the islands just a matter of time.

So why could the regiment not get clearance for Operation Backyard? All that day he had been trying to get an answer out of somebody, but all to no avail. As far as he could tell the operation had not been called off, but neither did anyone seem inclined to admit it was still on. Basically, no one seemed to want to talk about it at all.

Weighell poured himself a generous slug of malt whisky and gently simmered. He was beginning to wish they had pushed for an immediate insertion, rather than allow Brookes's patrol such a generous recovery period. But the Intelligence assessment was that ten undiscovered days on the mainland were the most they could reasonably hope for, and the general consensus at Northwood was that advance warning of air attacks would be most valuable during the actual landing operations on 21 and 22 May.

So they had agreed to insert the two patrols on the 14th. And now it was the evening of the 13th, and Whitehall and Northwood had become deaf to all enquiries. Weighell could imagine how the men on the *Resource* felt: waiting for the signal to go was bad enough when you knew it was definitely coming.

Who else could he ring? He could think of no one. After all, if the Prime Minister was pointedly not returning his calls, then who would?

He looked at the telephone, willing it to ring. And it did. In his haste to pick it up Weighell spilt most of his whisky across the table.

'Bryan?' a voice asked. It was Brigadier Mark Harringham from Northwood.

'Mark. I tried to get hold of you today.'

'That's why I am calling. I can guess what you want to know . . . I assume this is a secure line?'

'Yes.'

'Good. The answer is – we still don't know if Backyard is a starter, and if so when. The 14th seems unlikely . . .'

'Why, what's happened?'

'Politics, of course. The Foreign Minister threatened to resign if our troops were put ashore on the mainland before all the possibilities of the peace process – so called – had been exhausted.'

'Why didn't she let him?' Weighell asked angrily.

'Well, it's hard to say, but I'd guess that since the *Belgrano* she's been under a lot of pressure to at least go through all the right motions – diplomatically, that is. And of course he's on the other wing of the Party, and she only appointed him a month ago . . . he's in a strong position.'

'Ok, OK. But what's he waiting for? As far as I can see, all the proposals are dead in the water.'

'Not quite. Apparently, Galtieri's done a back somersault today; he told the UN chap – Pérez de Cuellar – that sovereignty is not a pre-condition for more talks. Of course, he's probably just playing for time, but Henderson and Parsons have been called back here from New York for more meetings, and we've been told not to rock the boat for a couple of days. No more *Belgrano*s and certainly no SAS adventures on the mainland.'

A couple of days, Weighell repeated to himself. He swore under his breath. 'So what do you think the chances are?'

'About 50–50, I'd say. She's still all for it, but she needs some help . . . preferably a statement from the Junta saying all bets are off and inviting us to do our worst.'

'Which isn't very likely.'

'Oh, I don't know. From what I can gather there doesn't seem to be much coherent policy-making going on over there. They might invade Chile – just for the hell of it.'

Weighell laughed, but his heart was not in it.

Raul was almost an hour late getting to the Rakosi, and Isabel had already drunk more than was sensible for her. Which was nothing unusual, she reminded herself. It might be the winter closing in, or being back in a place where heavy drinking was the norm, but she suspected her increasing level of consumption was inspired by a more personal malaise. She was drinking to blur the edges of deception. As well as self-deception, she added to herself, as Raul finally came in through the door.

His face broke into a smile when he saw her, as it always did. The same smile twisted a knife in her heart. But at least he was not falling in love with her. That night by the river, when he had sobbed out his fears, had thankfully put paid to the chance of any such relationship. It had opened the way for others – the older mistress or the older sister – and she had managed without much difficulty to steer him in the latter direction.

'My guardian angel,' he greeted her gaily, and she winced internally.

He seemed in a good mood and for half an hour they swapped small talk, his attention often distracted by the football match on the TV behind the bar. She told him what she had done that day – which was to check all the Rio Gallegos bus companies for their routes and fares – and what she was planning to do the next day: travel down the coast to investigate the local accommodation possibilities for tourists visiting the penguin colony at Cabo Virgenes.

He said he wished he could come with her, but some bigwig from Military Intelligence was arriving from Buenos Aires. 'Some Colonel named Solanille . . .'

The combination of shock and alcohol loosened her tongue. 'Tomas Solanille?' she blurted out.

He seemed not to notice the emotional charge which edged her voice. 'Yes, I think so. Why, have you heard of him?' he asked offhandedly, his eyes on the TV, where Racing Club had just been awarded a penalty.

'I think my uncle knows him,' she said steadily,

as the goalkeeper went one way, the ball the other. Major Tomas Solanille had been one of the men who had questioned her after her arrest: a cold, arrogant man, the sort who commissioned genealogical charts to advertise his good breeding. He had done nothing to her, except hand her over to the animals at the Naval Mechanical School.

Which was more than enough.

'Are you OK?' Raul asked.

She looked up guiltily. The football match had ended. 'Just tired,' she said.

'Too tired for our walk?' he asked, with the air of a small boy whose promised treat seemed in danger of disappearing.

'No,' she said, smiling. 'Some fresh air would be nice.'

It was fresher than she had expected, and for once taking his arm and snuggling up to his shoulder needed no more justification than the temperature and the chill breeze blowing across the estuary.

'It will soon be winter,' he said. 'I have never seen a winter in the south.'

'Maybe some agreement will be reached,' she suggested. 'Or we will win a quick victory,' she added, remembering that optimism was still the official order of the day.

He grunted. 'There might be an agreement,' he said seriously, 'but I don't think we can win a war with the English. I think we must prepare ourselves for the worst.' He turned suddenly to face her. 'Of course we will do our duty,' he added hastily, 'you must not ever think otherwise.'

'I know you will,' she said. 'But maybe there is still hope. The English are a long way from home . . .'

137

He explained the situation to her as he saw it, then added something almost as an aside: 'of course, we are saving our best hope for the moment when it will most matter.'

'What is that?' she asked.

He looked at her, and for a moment she thought something in her voice or her face had given her away, but what she had taken for suspicion turned into a rueful smile. 'The missile that sank their ship *Sheffield*, we have very few of them. We must make them all count.'

How many, she wanted to ask, but that would be too much. 'Have you one for each English ship?' she asked, almost playfully.

'If only,' he replied, and asked her how much longer her work would keep her in Rio Gallegos.

'A few more weeks,' she answered, and started listing what she still had to do. There was no way now that she could get a precise figure for the Exocets.

When they parted outside the Covadonga Hotel half an hour later he hugged her and kissed her lightly on the cheek. 'Thank you.'

'Thank you,' she replied.

'No, not for the evening,' he said, 'thank you for being my guardian angel.'

She walked upstairs, tears welling up in her eyes, and angrily threw her coat down on the bed. Then for what seemed liked a long time she sat in the only chair staring at the empty wall. Images from a film she had seen on British TV came into her mind, though at first she could see no reason why her memory had dragged them up. Someone – she thought it was Michael Caine – had been strapped into a chair, and was being subjected to a *mélange* of futuristic lights and sounds that were intended to scramble his psyche. But Michael Caine had managed to get a piece of glass – no, a nail – and was gouging it into his own hand to take his mind off the weird light-show.

And it worked.

It would work for her, she realized. But she did not need a nail, only a pen. She would start writing down what had happened to her, to all of them, all those years ago. How could the life of one sad-eyed pilot compete with the ghostly hordes of the dead and disappeared?

She would start now. This moment.

Giuseppe had been first. Giuseppe with the dancing brown hair and blue eyes. He had been a medical student, a lover of football and blonde girls and the poetry of Neruda. Every Tuesday, come rain, shine or bank robbery, he had visited his mother in her small apartment in La Boca, and told her fictional tales of the college life he had abandoned for the ERP. And one Tuesday he had been on his way back to Avellaneda, walking on the high girder bridge across the oil-stained waters of the Riachuelo, when the black car had stopped and swallowed him.

They had found him the next morning, in the woods at Ezeiza near the international airport, though it was only the valueless ring he had worn on one finger which had enabled an identification. The body was a charred hulk, held together by half-melted wire embedded in the charcoal crust of what had once been wrists and ankles. He would never trouble the sleep of the Junta again.

And none of his comrades had ever slept soundly again. Fear had taken their hearts, but they had carried on. They had not known how to stop.

Isabel put the pen aside and walked across to the window. The street was empty, the town sleeping. She wanted to wake every one of them, to scream at them: 'Where were you when Giuseppe Trappatoni died?'

It had worked, she realized. Raul's life or death no longer seemed to weigh so heavily on the scales.

She went to bed and managed to sleep for a few hours. As dawn showed outside she went for a walk through the empty town, down to the riverside park. The sun was rising above the mouth of the estuary, throwing a line of reflected light along the centre of the wide river, between the anchored freighters. Behind her an oil tanker rumbled along Calle Orkeke.

Isabel remembered another tanker, another early morning. In Córdoba four of them had invaded a dairy depot, all wearing red masks, and hijacked a milk tanker. Then they had driven it to the Sarmiento shanty town, and dispensed milk by the bucketful to people who could not have afforded to fill a thimble. The looks on their faces had been worth a thousand theories.

They had mounted a similar operation a month later – only this time it had been a lumber company they had held up. Building materials had been stashed aboard lorries, and driven out to another shanty town, where families lived in homes made from packing cases. There too they were greeted as deliverers, if only from rain through the roof.

She had been telling that man in London the truth when she said she felt no guilt. On the contrary, she felt proud of everything they had tried to do, and sometimes done. Her comrades might all be dead, and the Junta still alive, but they had not died in vain. None of them. They had brought hope, no matter how short-lived; and they had demonstrated a simple humanity when such demonstrations invited a lonely and painful death.

And if she had any say in the matter, then one day they would get the recognition they deserved.

Please let this be good news, Weighell told himself as he climbed the last few stairs on his way to Conference Room B. The men gathered round the table were not quite the same as on the previous occasion. The FO's Latin-American expert was absent, as was Air-Marshal Railton. And this time Cecil Matheson was flanked by his superior, the grey-haired, weasel-faced Foreign Minister.

Weighell's first impression was that the latter looked thoroughly pissed off. Which probably did mean good news, he told himself.

The MI6 man, Anthony Sharp, looked full of the joys of spring, but that could just be congenital idiocy. Harringham appeared his usual cheerful self, while the MOD's Dennis Eckersley seemed more bored than anything. Weighell thought he could detect the faintest of knowing smirks on Cecil Matheson's lips.

There was no mistaking the Prime Minister's mood. The eyes had a definite glint to them, and the mouth showed about as much warmth as a Venus fly-trap. 'Good morning, gentlemen,' she said coldly. 'There is only one item of business to deal with – Operation Backyard.' She glanced at her Foreign Minister, and received a bleak stare in return.

She asked Weighell to explain the reasons why any further delay would severely reduce the value of the operation. He explained them. Harringham was asked to concur, and did so. The PM then outlined the Foreign Minister's objections, rather than let him do so himself. Such an operation might compromise the last chance of peace, she said, with about as much conviction as an English batsman facing the West Indian bowlers.

It was like watching a child tearing the limbs off a spider, Weighell thought, and for a fleeting moment felt almost sorry for the Foreign Minister.

Matheson provided the *coup de grâce* to his own boss, with some assistance from the beaming Sharp. Intelligence agents in New York – exactly whose agents was not specified – had managed to bug the Argentinian Consulate, and to record one end of a conversation between the Argentinian envoy to the UN and General Galtieri. This conversation – and other scraps recorded in the Consulate – clearly showed that the Argentinian Government had abandoned any hopes they might have had of reaching an agreement with the British which they could sell to their own people. The Junta's only remaining interest lay in putting off the evil day, in buying all the time that they possibly could in the forlorn hope that something somehow might provide the miracle needed for their own salvation.

'I believe this removes all the objections to proceeding with Operation Backyard,' the Prime Minister concluded. The Foreign Minister gave her a look which Weighell could only interpret as pure hatred, and muttered his acquiescence.

The silence in the newspapers was ominous, Isabel thought. The chance of peace was gone; now the Junta was just waiting for the blow to fall. She wondered if any of the uniformed idiots still thought they had any chance of victory, or if they were all just paralysed by the prospect of imminent defeat.

It was a raw, cold day, and the Patagonian steppe looked even more inhospitable than usual. Out in the distance, swirls of dust hovered in the wind like miniature tornadoes, while closer to the road the dry clumps of grass were being tugged this way and that with a violent intensity. Away to her left two small dark clouds had dropped out of the overall grey to mount guard over the blunt peak of Mount Aymond.

Maybe she would write a guidebook when this was all over, she thought. She was rapidly accumulating all the necessary information, and if such books needed their authors to have a feel for the area in question, then she thought she was well qualified. In Ushuaia there was a Museum of the End of the World, and it was not just a matter of geography. There was something about southern Patagonia and southern Chile that almost revelled in the idea of being a long way from anywhere else.

'Don't they know it's the end of the world – it ended when I lost your love,' she sang to herself. If she had anything to thank Michael for, then it was an education in English and American rock music.

No, that wasn't fair, she thought. He had tried to understand her.

The road went into a long curve around an outflung shoulder of the distant mountain. At the point where it straightened once more a car was parked off the road, and as she went past it pulled out onto the road behind her. She felt a sharp stab of anxiety, and a lightness in her stomach. In the rear mirror she saw the car accelerate to pass her.

She turned, heart in mouth, to glance at the driver and was relieved to find that it was Andrew Lawson, who she had last seen three weeks before in Punta Arenas. If he had come across the border in person, it had to be something important.

'We need to talk,' he shouted through the window. 'I'll pull up when we have a decent view in both directions.'

He pulled off the tarmac at a spot close to her bridge, where any approaching traffic would be visible at least a mile away. She left the road behind him and got out of the car. He was walking towards her with a gun in his hand.

Her heart sank.

'Have you got a spare tyre?' he asked.

'What? Well, yes . . .'

He took aim and squeezed the trigger. Her left front tyre exhaled noisily. 'So I've stopped to help a lady in distress,' he said with a smile. 'I take it you can play the helpless woman if you have to.'

'As well as you can play the moronic male,' she retorted. She felt really angry at him for scaring her like that. Only a man who had seen too many films and not enough reality could do something so stupid.

He was already retrieving her jack from the boot, oblivious to her anger. She decided to let it fade away. After all, how could an Englishman be expected to know anything about fear?

She looked up and down the highway. It was empty. 'Shall I put the stuff in your car?' she asked.

'Good idea,' he said, unfastening the second bolt. 'Just put it under the front seat.'

'Won't they check your car at the border?' she asked. It had occurred to her that if he got caught she probably would too. And he would probably have diplomatic immunity.

'It had occurred to me,' he said mildly, hearing the implied criticism.

'Yes, OK. I just . . .'

'I have a false compartment in the door,' he said. 'Real James Bond stuff.'

'What about the rear-mounted machine-guns?' she asked drily.

''Fraid not. Budget cutbacks, probably.'

'What do we need to talk about?' she asked pointedly.

'Ah, yes. The purpose of this little tête-à-tête in the Patagonian wastes. Some of our soldiers will be dropping in nearby in the not-too-distant future. In fact, they may well be here already – my boss hadn't been given the precise date when I last spoke to him. There's . . .'

'You mean here on the mainland?' she asked incredulously.

'Ummm, yes. Only a few men, I believe. They will be watching your airbase at Rio Gallegos for planes taking off, and so on. Under cover, of course.'

She found it hard to believe, though after a few moments' thought she could see no overwhelming arguments against such an operation. The next thing that occurred to her was how this might affect her own mission. 'You're not expecting me to take them breakfast each morning, are you?' she asked belligerently.

'No. But in the event of an emergency London thought it advisable that you should know of each other's existence.'

'What?'

'It makes sense, don't you think?'

'But what could they do for me? What could I do for them, come to that?'

'They could get you out of Argentina when they go. On a submarine, I presume, though I don't know. As for what you could do for them . . .' He shrugged.

'I could hardly hide them under my hotel bed,' she said sarcastically.

'You could perhaps help them get to the border,' he said reasonably. 'I don't know. Like I said: it just seemed sensible to give both you and them another possible option. That's all.'

'It also gives us both someone else to betray,' she said. 'What do they know about me?'

'Only your name and the hotel you're staying at. And they wouldn't betray you.'

'Why, because they're English gentlemen?'

'Because there'd be no reason for the Argentinian military to ask them.'

'You probably don't have many torturers who enjoy their work in England,' she said coldly. 'Are you going to give me the name of their hotel?'

'No, but I'm going to show you on the map the general area where they'll be holed up.'

She looked at him in amazement. 'And then what? You expect me to wander round the local countryside looking for a bunch of men in a hole reading the *Sun*?'

6

Aboard the *Resource* they had received word that the operation was to begin shortly before midnight on Saturday 15 May. The eleven men most concerned were told first thing the next morning, and a frantic day's preparations ensued. The supplies and signalling equipment were checked through once more; the weaponry given a final test fire from the ship's rails. Last-minute letters were composed, decisions on personal gear taken and retaken, nerves kept under control by the constant banter.

That morning the eight men of the two patrols – 'North' under Docherty, 'South' under Brookes – were introduced to the Sea King crewmen: Lieutenants Billings and Hatchard, and Petty-Officer Crabtree. This threesome seemed to be under the impression that they were going on a fortnight's camping holiday in Chile, and Hatchard asked the others what they thought about taking a hamper with them for the inevitable picnics. All three of them, the SAS men decided, were 'OK for the Navy'.

Docherty remembered the hamper as he stepped out onto the rolling deck shortly after ten-thirty that evening, and smiled to himself. The *Resource* was still making good headway into the west, and seemed to be showing fewer lights than usual. With all the modern detection equipment available, Docherty knew, it still counted for something to be hard to see in the dark. It was probably his imagination, but he felt he could feel the tension aboard the ship, accompanying this dark, silent voyage towards the enemy coast.

They might still be in the self-proclaimed exclusion zone, but they were a long way from help, and the moment the helicopter was airborne the *Resource* would be heading back towards the relative safety of the Task Force with all the speed its engines could muster.

The Sea King HC4 was waiting for them on the flight deck, its newly acquired extra fuel tanks adding to the ungainliness of its silhouette. Inside it had been stripped of all but the essentials, and maybe a few of those.

'It looks like a burglar's been in,' Razor observed.

'They've even taken the seats out,' Stanley complained.

'We have a normal range of 480 kilometres,' Lieutenant Billings announced, 'and we're probably travelling 700. I'm afraid we can't even carry your normal supply of bullshit.'

'They get testy when you complain,' Hedge noticed.

'Probably his time of the month,' Wacko murmured, and found himself thinking about Anne.

'It would have been more comfortable if they'd fired us at Argentina from a cannon,' Stanley said, grabbing a piece of fuselage floor to park himself on.

'They'll probably send us back that way,' Hedge said.

The nervous chatter continued until the door slid shut, whereupon a brief interlude of silence accompanied the helicopter's ascent from the moving deck.

According to the weather report the low-hanging bank of clouds above them extended all the way to the Argentinian coast, and would at least reduce the chances of their being spotted by the naked eye. There was also a stiff wind blowing out of the west, buffeting the helicopter and ensuring a far from easy ride.

Spread around the walls of the Sea King's belly the eight SAS men could see nothing of the outside world, and it seemed an eternity before Crabtree passed back the information that the coast was in sight. Docherty's North patrol began preparing themselves, stretching limbs, checking, for the umpteenth time, that all fastenings were secure, and running narrow-beam torches over each other's make-up.

'Try not to kiss each other too often in the first few hours,' Stanley advised them.

'He still thinks he's in West Bromwich,' Wacko said.

'One minute,' Crabtree told them, and almost before the words were out they were settling down onto Argentinian soil.

'Do you think they're still angry about Rattin and Alf Ramsey?' Razor asked.

'I would be,' Docherty said, as Brookes pulled back the door for them and let the wind in. A flat expanse stretched away into darkness.

The four men leapt down one by one, feeling the weight of their bergens as they landed.

'Good luck, lads,' Brookes shouted above the roar of the blades, gave them one last wave and slid the door shut. The Sea King lifted off into the cloudy sky, and flew off towards the south, leaving the patrol alone in a silence that was broken only by the wind and in almost total darkness.

Assuming that they had been put down in the right spot, they were about six miles in from the coast and roughly 25 south-west of the Rio Gallegos airbase. The countryside around them was virtually treeless steppe, which sloped gently up towards a line of low hills some 10 miles to the west. It was almost as empty of people as the Falklands, and almost as full of sheep.

For the moment, this was all hearsay, and the patrol was forced to rely for direction solely on its two illuminated compasses. Ben led off, followed in fairly close formation by fellow Scotsman Docherty, and Wacko and Razor. Each man carried a silenced MP5 sub-machine-gun cradled in his arms, a 9mm Browning High Power handgun and a favoured knife on his person.

Unlike Brookes's patrol, North had elected not to further burden themselves with more esoteric weapons. Docherty was a believer in sticking to basics unless there was a good reason not to, and since no members of his patrol shared Hedge's skill with a crossbow he had deemed it wiser to travel without one.

They were carrying more than enough, he thought, and increased mobility was usually worth a slight reduction in the range of fire-power at a patrol's disposal. But there was no set answer. Brookes had judged differently, and only time would tell who was right on this occasion. Maybe both of them. One thing was certain: it was too late for either of them to change his mind.

The thought of the woman crossed Docherty's mind. Hemmings had made a bad mistake in telling both patrols about her at the final briefing that morning – there had been no sense in giving her name and address to South, who would almost certainly never come within 100 miles of her. If one or all of Brookes's South patrol was captured and tortured – which was hardly out of the question given all they knew about the Junta – then she had been needlessly endangered.

Docherty had not said anything at the time – the younger men were wired up enough as it was – but he had been surprised by such an elementary error. Nor had he much liked the idea of her knowing of their existence: for all he knew she was incompetent enough to get herself caught and tortured. It had happened once. He thought about what Hemmings had told them about her: college student, urban guerrilla, tortured prisoner, exile. The only one the Intelligence Services had managed to persuade to work for them. She had to be special, he decided, one way or the other.

He would like to meet her. Since his time in Mexico he had come to realize that distance was a great aid in understanding one's own country, and he would have liked to hear what she had to say about Argentina since her exile and return.

He would like to meet her, but not on this trip. This time around he had no desire to talk Spanish with anyone but the sheep. And according to Razor many Patagonian sheep spoke only Welsh. Docherty smiled and checked his watch. They had been walking an hour.

Up ahead of him Ben was in his element. The wind, the smell of clean air, that sense of space which even near-zero visibility could not hide – it all seemed a far cry from the Hereford barracks or the crowded hold of the *Resource*, far more akin to the vast silence of Lochaber and the Great Glen. All the bustle and the restrictions and the pettiness were gone. All the artificiality. They were in the middle of nowhere, and at the centre of everything.

At the rear of the column Razor's thoughts were rather less cosmic. The Cup Final was only six days away, which seemed far too short a time to win the war and get Ossie Ardiles back to England. It would be the eighth time Spurs had been to Wembley since his birth, and the first visit he would miss seeing, though admittedly he had been a bit young to appreciate the Cup Finals in '61 and '62. His mother even claimed he had slept through the former, but that was hard to believe, even of a three-year-old supporter.

At least the coming Saturday's game would be on the World Service, and he would be able to listen in on earphones, provided they did not need the radio for anything trivial, like warning the Task Force of a massed Exocet attack.

Fifteen feet in front of Razor, and only just visible in the gloom, Wacko was still trying to drive thoughts of Anne and Brendan from his mind. The truly horrible part was that while the thought of her having sex with someone else, of her letting some other man slide his dick inside her, produced a sinking feeling in the pit of Wacko's stomach, he was simultaneously asking himself whether he was still in love with her. Alone of the four SAS men walking across the Patagonian steppe, Wacko would have almost welcomed some sort of impediment to their progress. Anything to take his mind off his beloved wife.

After dropping off North patrol the Sea King had

swung sharply south, crossing the Chilean border and continuing across the wide expanse of Lomas Bay, which separates the south-eastern corner of the South American mainland from the volcanic island of Tierra del Fuego.

Once over the island, the Sea King crew kept their craft some six miles to the neutral western side of the Chile–Argentine border, which bisects the island from north to south. Forty minutes later they turned abruptly east, back across the border into Argentina. Ten minutes more and they were putting the chopper down onto a stretch of meadowland some 18 miles to the west of Rio Grande.

Like the members of North before then, Brookes's men jumped down onto enemy soil, but from this point on their experiences began to diverge. An hour had passed, they were 100 miles further to the south, and the low cloud cover had begun to break up, revealing patches of starlit sky and vastly increasing ground-level visibility.

Like most things in life, Brookes thought, this was both a plus and a minus. But, remembering that dreadful first march through the mist on West Falkland, he was inclined to look on the sanguine side. At least it would make some sort of change, being able to see where they were going.

And the further they could see, the less paranoid they needed to be about making noise. 'Ready?' he asked. 'Then let's go.'

The land sloped down from north to south, and the four men set off on a south-easterly course, which was intended to take them slowly down to the Rio Moneta. Following this would bring them to a confluence with the Rio Grande, and five miles downstream from that they should encounter the bridge which carried the island's main road across the neck of the river's estuary. A turn to the left would take them into the town of Rio Grande; a turn to the right towards the airbase.

All four men were enjoying themselves after the cramped noisiness of the helicopter, mostly from the pure sense of release, but also from the simple satisfaction that came from confidence. Each man was thinking that they had been through it all before: the marches and the scrapes, the bored and cramped hours in the OP. The wet, the cold, Hedge's farts. What could Tierra del Fuego throw at them that West Falkland had not? It even seemed drier, and anything less than an inch of water in your boots had to count as luxury.

The Sea King had reversed its aerial tracks, crossing the border into Chilean Tierra del Fuego at almost the same spot it had entered Argentina. The sky above and to the west was now clear, a moon shining somewhere behind them, and ahead to their left they could see the forested slopes of the Pico Nose, the glow of it's snow-capped peak shining in the moonlight.

'How are we doing for fuel?' Crabtree asked.

'Looks OK. We can make Dawson Island, at any rate.'

The Sea King flew on, across grass-covered hills and the black waters of the Whiteside Channel, which separates Dawson Island from Tierra del Fuego.

'Doesn't look very inviting,' Lieutenant Hatchard remarked, as they flew across the dark forested island. 'I'd guess we have enough fuel to reach the mainland.'

'How much of a guess is that?' his fellow lieutenant, Billings, wanted to know. 'The island looks a damn sight more inviting than the sea.'

'I'm pretty certain. And they wanted us as far away from the drop zones as possible.'

'So they did,' Billings agreed, only a hint of irony in his voice.

The Sea King ventured out over water once more, this time the famous Strait of Magellan. The three Navy men watched in silence as the fuel indicator stopped even bothering to flicker and the Chilean mainland inched steadily towards them. Ten minutes later they cleared the coastline and the coastal track, and Billings brought the helicopter down in a convenient clearing some 200 yards inland.

For most of a minute the three men sat in silence, savouring their safe arrival. It was 0220 hours on 17 May.

They removed their gear and, thinking to minimize the conflagration, tried to drain the remaining fuel from the tanks. There was none. Another half a mile and they would not have needed to destroy the helicopter.

As it was, they had to pile forest undergrowth into the Sea King to make sure of its destruction. As flames danced through the cab and hold, they turned away and started trekking up the hill, towards their intended camp-site.

None of them had noticed Juan Fonseca watching from the trees. He had been walking home along the coastal track from a friend's house after a long and particularly satisfying game of chess. It had been satisfying because he had beaten his friend for the first time in months, and it was perhaps the resultant sense of well-being which persuaded him to investigate the strange sight of a helicopter landing in the forest.

It was not something which became clearer as he drew near. He arrived to see the crew of three – Englishmen from the Falklands War, judging by their faces and the strange markings on the helicopter – setting fire to the craft they had just arrived in. They had then smiled at each other and taken off into the forest like backpackers.

Fonseca went to look at the helicopter, now burning rather desultorily, but could make no sense of the business. He walked back to the coastal track, and wondered what he should do.

Nothing, he decided. He could make the trip into Punta Arenas the next day and tell the authorities, but he could see no good reason why he should. Wednesday was his day for visiting the town, and the helicopter was going nowhere. The three Englishmen might be invading Chile, but somehow he doubted it. This had to be something to do with their war with Argentina, and where that was concerned he rather favoured the English. They, after all, were not always threatening Chile, the way Argentina was.

On board the *Resource* Bill Hemmings spent the night waiting nervously in the ship's radio room beside the brand new PRC319. Every now and then he would reach over and brush an imaginary speck of dust off one of the gleaming surfaces. Sod's Law being in force, the first signal arrived while he was out of the room collecting cups of tea for himself and the orderly, an anorexic-looking young chap from Liverpool.

It came as a written message on the screen: NORTH BEDDED DOWN FOR THE NIGHT . . .

OPERATION PROCEEDING AS PLANNED ...
OUT.

'Any reply, sir, or shall I just acknowledge receipt?'
the orderly asked Hemmings.

'Just acknowledge,' Hemmings said. It was the first
time he had seen the PRC319 in operation, and he was
impressed. Hemmings was also pleased that the sender
– either Docherty or Wacknadze – had not felt himself
constrained by past SAS practice to use the system's
burst-message Morse capability. The PRC319 evaded
transmission detection by picking out frequencies at
random from a wide range, and North's sender had
just demonstrated both an understanding of, and his
confidence in, the new technology.

Hemmings was still feeling pleased about this when
South reported in, using the burst-message Morse
facility. Either Brookes or Moseley obviously lacked
such confidence. It was most likely Brookes. Moseley
had seemed both intrigued and delighted by the new
system, but his PC was probably getting more cautious
and more set in his ways as he got older.

The message, when translated, was the same. South
was also bedded down.

A few minutes later the Sea King crew reported
their safe landing and their current location a few
miles further inland. They had taken the helicopter as
far from the SAS patrols as anyone could have hoped.
So far, so good, Hemmings told himself. The SAS
invasion of Argentina was going according to plan.

That morning dawned clear and cold over the Rio
Grande valley in Tierra del Fuego, cloudy and cold
over the grassy steppe south of Rio Gallegos on the
mainland. Both patrols were secure in their scrapes

half an hour before dawn, and the daylight hours passed without any great alarm. Better visibility had given South a safer location, high on a grassy slope beneath overhanging rocks in an empty valley. Dawn had been unkind enough to reveal a road not 200 yards from the North scrapes, but during the course of the day only four vehicles made use of it.

With darkness both patrols moved on. Each had a reasonably specific location in mind for their OP, but both were aware of the limitations of the maps they were carrying, and knew that their final decisions would have to await an inspection *in situ*.

Docherty's patrol had the longer journey that night, but also the easier one, and soon after 0200 they could see, with the aid of the telescope, the lights of Rio Gallegos three or four miles away to the north, and those of the airbase some two and a half miles away to the north-west. Within an hour they had picked out a likely spot for the OP and begun to excavate. If daylight showed a better or safer vantage point they would move house again the following night.

Brookes's patrol had a more difficult time. The area they needed to traverse was criss-crossed by tracks, contained several farms, and, according to the plethora of signs, was an area much frequented by anglers. They took it slowly and circuitously, aware that even one barking dog might pull the world down on top of them, and midnight had passed before they slipped across the main road and into the area of rough grassland north of the river estuary. The few lights of the town were visible away to the north-east, but the only visible evidence of the airbase came with a helicopter, which flew low and noisily over their heads before disappearing northwards.

It was almost 0430 before the patrol had worked its way round to a position between the airbase and the sea, and a provisional placement for the OP had to be swiftly agreed if the four men were to be safely out of sight by dawn.

More by luck than judgement, the location proved an ideal one. The area proved less flat than the map had suggested, more like a miniature landscape of hills and valleys, with the former rarely rising more than 10 feet and the latter seldom more than 10 feet wide. The OP was set on the eastern slope of a shallow dip on the edge of this strange countryside, and though it offered no direct view of the airbase a mile to the west, it did provide, as they soon discovered, a panoramic view of the sky above it. No planes would be taking off or landing without their knowledge.

Daylight on 18 May brought North rather less satisfactory news. Planes took off from Rio Gallegos airbase on a north-westerly course, and circled round behind the distant estuary before heading eastwards out to sea. The patrol was simply too far away from the airbase for precise observation. All through that day they filed as accurate a log of air-traffic movements as they could, but once darkness arrived they would have to move nearer and take up the digging tools once more.

Outside the Rio Grande airbase, Brookes had more adventurous plans. His patrol had also been monitoring traffic in and out, but so far they had seen neither Super Etendards nor Mirages, and Brookes decided a closer inspection of the airbase was in order. Shortly after midnight he and Stanley left a sleeping Hedge and an alert Mozza, and started working their way across the pocked grassland towards the airbase perimeter.

They moved slowly, frequently stopping for several minutes to listen for a possible patrol, but the only unnatural sounds came from motor vehicles, either around the airbase or on the road beyond it. Soon the yellow lights of the distant control tower were visible above the grassy knolls, and a further quarter of a mile brought them to where the land suddenly turned flatter, as if some enormous steamroller had been employed. Lying face down behind the final fold, the two men took turns examining the airbase through their image-intensifying night-sight.

About 50 yards ahead of them a tall wire fence, topped with razor wire but apparently not electrified, ran out of sight to both left and right. One hundred and fifty yards behind this fence, and parallel to it, a single runway stretched half a mile or more in each direction on a roughly east-west axis. Between fence and runway there was nothing but rough grass waving in the wind.

The only planes parked in the open were two Aeromacchi reconnaissance craft and a single Puma helicopter. All the others were presumably tucked up for the night in the long line of buildings on the far side, between the runway and the distant highway. Away to the left there were four identical long, one-storey buildings, which looked distinctly like barracks. Next in line to the west were a two-storey office building, several large cylindrical fuel tanks, what looked like a civilian terminal building, and three hangars of various sizes. The doors of the nearest one was open, revealing the front half of a Skyhawk.

Most interesting of all, almost directly opposite the SAS men's position, three concrete shelters in the shape of flat-roofed pyramids had been constructed, and foundations dug for three more. The doors of each were shut. Working on the theory that people gave the best protection to what they valued most, Brookes reckoned the shelters might well contain Super Etendards, Exocets or both. If they did . . .

Brookes took a deep breath. If they did, he could see very little in the way of their strolling over and blowing the planes into little pieces.

Getting away would not be so simple, of course.

Stanley's hand touched his arm, and he followed the Brummie's glance to the right. The night-sight showed a patrol of four Argentinian soldiers wandering lackadaisically along the outside of the perimeter fence, chatting.

They ambled slowly past, never even throwing so much as a glance in the SAS men's direction. As I was thinking, Brookes said to himself. It looked almost too easy.

In Rio Gallegos, on the following morning, Isabel Fuentes popped the last corner of the cinnamon pastry into her mouth and stared out of the wide front window of the Le Croissant patisserie at the rain sweeping across the intersection of Calles Estrada and Zapiola. On the opposite corner a Pinguino Company bus was slowly consuming a queue of waiting passengers, all of whom were attempting to shield themselves from the downpour with soggy newspapers held above their heads. As was usual in such situations, the driver, happily ensconced in his dry seat, seemed to be checking each ticket as if it was a forgery.

Isabel smiled, took a sip of the excellent coffee, and

went back to her newspaper's reporting of the Junta's final rejection of the British peace proposals. She could see that they had little choice in the matter – assuming that they wanted to save any face at all – but when all was said and done they were only prolonging the agony. And killing off the nation's young men in the process.

She folded the newspaper and stared out once more at the rain. This was not the day she should have chosen for a day off, she decided, but since the job itself was imaginary it hardly seemed worth worrying about. After almost a month's work the briefcase on the chair beside her was bulging with information for the discerning tourist, including a glowing write-up for the establishment she was currently patronizing – 'the best croissants south of Bahia Blanca', no less.

She smiled inwardly, and wondered how much longer this would go on. She had enough money for another six months – British Intelligence was either absurdly generous or had no idea of the Patagonian cost of living – although she felt she could not stand much more than another one in the Covadonga.

She would never have guessed it, but she missed cooking. Eating out all the time was not only boring; it became almost soul-destroying after a while. There were some things people needed to do for themselves, she decided, if they wanted to keep in touch with who they were. Maybe that was why the rich tended to lose touch, because they never did their own cooking.

There were compensations in all the free time offered by hotel life. Reading, for one: she seemed to be consuming novels at the rate of one a day, or one every two for the longer ones. She had a feeling that the small secondhand bookshop in

Calle Urquiza had not seen a better customer since TV arrived in town.

She took another sip of the strong dark coffee and wondered whether to have another pastry. There was no point in leaving until the rain abated.

A large limousine drew up at the kerb almost directly opposite her window-seat, splashing water from the swollen gutter onto the pavement. The rear door opened and two legs emerged, swiftly followed by the rest of Tomas Solanille. His hair was greyer than she remembered, but the aquiline nose and the bleak eyes were unmistakable. She almost cried out in her surprise.

Another man emerged from the driving seat on the far side, younger, with that lean, cadaverous look which she always associated with Colombian gangsters on American TV shows. The two of them hurried up the short flight of steps and into the patisserie. Sit at the back, she mentally urged them, but to no avail. They sat down at the only empty window table, just as the man occupying the table between her and them got up to leave. Only two other tables were occupied, both by pairs of women, and they were in the centre of the room.

Isabel felt exposed, frightened and close to panic. If he should recognize her . . .

At least he had sat down with his back to her. Keep calm, she told herself. Remember the old discipline.

Would he know her after all this time? She had recognized him, but that was different – she had been questioned by only one of him, whereas he had doubtless questioned hundreds like her. In a way she hoped he would recognize her . . .

Christ, she told herself, get a grip! This was not the

time or the place for restoring her faith in humanity. This was something to be got out of, as quickly as possible, as quietly as possible. As alive as possible.

It was a hell of a long way to the door. And first she had to pay the bill. Christ, she thought, that would have been a smart move – being chased into the street by the woman at the counter for not paying.

She got to her feet, took the briefcase in one hand and the newspaper in the other, and, turning in such a way that her face was never visible to the two men, went up to the counter and paid her bill. Then, taking a deep breath, she walked across the five yards separating her from the door, half-hiding her head with the newspaper, as if preparing to protect herslef from the rain outside.

The only problem with this was that it left no free hand to open the door. Solanille obliged, extending an arm to push it open, without even bothering to glance up at her face.

She emerged into the rain, shivering with the memory of fear.

Early on the morning of Wednesday 19 May Juan Fonseca started up his battered Dodge pick-up and drove the nine miles up the coastal track to the Chilean town of Punta Arenas. He had several things to pick up at the market, and it always paid to buy early, so it was not until nearly noon that he walked through the portals of the police station on the corner of Calles Errazuriz and Navarro. Once inside he had some trouble persuading the duty officer to take his story seriously, but the fortuitous arrival of an officer who knew Fonseca, and was ready to vouch for his reliability, saw the wheels of investigation grinding into motion. The local military base was informed, and a meeting of all parties arranged on the southern outskirts of town. From there a convoy of police and military vehicles followed the battered pick-up down the coastal track.

It was soon being shadowed by several other vehicles, each containing a journalist alerted by his or her informant in the ranks of the police and military. By the time the convoy reached that spot on the coast nearest to the burnt-out Sea King, it contained nine vehicles. A veritable swarm of people, uniformed and otherwise, poured up through the trees to examine the scene in the clearing.

Fonseca and various officers were exhaustively interviewed, photographs were taken, theories propounded. By mid-afternoon the more seasoned journalists were back in Punta Arenas, phone in hand, trying to sell the story to the nationals in Santiago and the international press associations. News of the helicopter's landing might have taken some 60 hours to cover the eight miles to Punta Arenas, but it only required a couple more to reach Buenos Aires and London.

From the latter it rebounded southwards, via Ascension, to the Task Force. Hemmings heard of the discovery as dusk was falling across the scattered ships of the fleet, and immediately signalled the two patrols on Argentinian soil.

For Docherty the news explained quite a lot. Half an hour earlier two lorryloads of army troops had arrived at the Rio Gallegos airbase, and in the meantime two helicopters had been flying obvious search patterns over the hills to their left. Despite the fact that the Sea

King had been discovered more than 100 miles away, someone in enemy intelligence had clearly put two and two together. If the helicopter had put down troops in Argentina, then the obvious place to look for them was outside the prime targets for reconnaissance – the two major airbases. Hence the arrival of the lorries.

At least it was getting dark. Docherty doubted whether an exhaustive search would begin before first light the next day, although the Argentinians might send out random patrols that night, particularly if they had access to thermal-imaging equipment.

He took another long look at the airbase through the telescope. Both helicopters had now landed, and the troops had mostly disappeared into one of the barracks buildings. The patrol was safe for the moment, but Docherty reckoned their chances of remaining undiscovered for another twenty-four hours were less than even. If they stayed where they were.

He turned to Ben. 'Wake the others,' he said.

When all four of them were gathered together, each lying in his own arm of the cross-shaped hide, faces only a foot or so apart in the central space, Docherty told the others of the Sea King's discovery, recounted developments in the airbase below, and asked for suggestions.

Razor came up with the same idea as Docherty himself. 'Why not move back to the other OP, at least for the day? We couldn't see what was happening from up there, even with a half-decent telescope, so with any luck they'll not bother extending their search that far out.'

'I agree,' Docherty said. He raised an eyebrow at the other two, who both nodded their acquiescence. 'Ok. I think we should move as soon as it's dark enough, or

166

even slightly sooner, before they start thinking about trying out their image intensifiers. So you two start clearing up here while Wacko calls home and tells them what we're doing.'

'Right, boss.'

Docherty resumed his watch, and noted down the return of an Acromacchi reconnaissance plane. Behind him Wacko was tapping lightly on the PRC 319's keypad, while Razor and Ben were gathering up the patrol's gear. He had to admit it, Docherty told himself: coping with life behind enemy lines was a damn sight easier than coping with life at home.

A hundred miles to the south Brookes's patrol had received the same news of the Sea King's discovery, and drawn some of the same conclusions. They too had witnessed an upsurge in helicopter activity over the environs of the base, and although the siting of their hide precluded any knowledge of arriving troops, the prospect of such had entered their heads before Docherty's info was relayed on to them by Hemmings.

The major difference in their situation concerned the surrounding terrain. From what they had been able to gather, the area of pocked, lunar grassland seemed to cover at least a dozen square miles. Searching it thoroughly would require both a very large number of men and an inordinate amount of time. The odds against their being found seemed good to Brookes, and the others concurred.

To pull back, as North was doing, seemed more dangerous than staying put. There was nothing behind them but more of the same and the sea. To reach relative safety they would have to move back inland, along the same difficult route through populated country they had used on their way in.

The clinching argument, though, was the existence of the concrete aircraft shelters. Brookes suspected they contained Super Etendards, and unless and until he discovered otherwise the PC could see no justification for removing the patrol from its observation duties. When those planes took to the skies the Task Force would have to be waiting for them, or who knew what fresh disaster might occur.

South would sit out any search.

7

The following day clouds filled the skies over both airbases. From North's original OP, Razor watched through the telescope as the Argentinian troops conducted a systematic sweep of the hills around the airbase. A long interval of rain did nothing to quicken their step, and after a while Razor began to feel almost sorry for the bedraggled lines in the distance.

The rain must also have helped mask the edges of their second OP, because the line of troops edged its way past the turfed-over roof of the empty hide without a second glance.

The whole scene reminded Razor of the hunt across the heather in the original film of *The Thirty-Nine Steps*. Even the countryside looked similar. He wondered if he might end up like Richard Hannay, handcuffed to a beautiful woman. Some hope, he thought. Some fucking hope.

A hundred miles to the south, Hedge was wondering whether there was a pizza delivery service in Rio Grande and coming up with much the same answer. The rain was falling on South as well, and with rather more venom.

As for the real enemy, the helicopters had been active overhead again that morning, but no Argentinian

troops had so far crossed the OP's line of vision.
Which did not mean very much. In such country,
and in such a noisy downpour, they could be 20
yards away and nobody would know the difference.
Hedge was not fond of this particular site: he would
have preferred one with a wider field of vision, even
at the inevitable cost of greater visibility. It was just
too nerve-racking, not being able to see anything.

Still, Brookes was a good bloke and a much more
experienced soldier than he was, so . . .

'Penny for 'em,' Mozza whispered to his left. One
advantage of the rain was that it made whispered
conversation safe.

'I was just wondering what Johnny Gaucho's doing
out there.'

'Probably drinking hot tea in front of the canteen
TV,' Mozza said.

'Go on, rub it in.'

Soon after dusk, Brookes decided they needed a check
on what was happening at the airbase. Stanley and
Mozza were dispatched, travelling light, wearing
PNGs and with only their Browning High Powers
for armament.

Shortly after they had left, a message from Hemmings
came through: the landing force would be hitting
the Falklands beaches the following morning. 'Just
thought you'd like to know,' Hemmings signed off,
but Brookes, mulling over the message, wondered
whether the Green Slime man was obliquely trying
to say something else. Something like: 'if you're going
to have a go at those Super Es, then tonight would be
the night to do it.'

But if they had a go and failed, then who would be

170

there to give advanced warning of the planes' arrival over the Task Force?

And yet, and yet ... The Argentinian security looked pathetic, the chances of success good. He still had a couple of hours to make up his mind.

Mozza and Stanley, meanwhile, had reached that vantage point which Brookes and Stanley had occupied two nights before, and removed the PNGs. The scene looked much the same to Stanley, except for the fact that all three of the concrete shelters were now open. And inside each one, brilliantly illuminated in white fluorescent light, stood a gleaming Super Etendard jet. 'Geronimo,' he muttered under his breath.

'There's another two parked outside the far hangar,' Mozza whispered, handing him the night-sight.

Stanley saw them for himself. Four Skyhawks were lined up behind them. The two Aeromacchis were parked in the same place as they had been before. The helicopter had acquired a twin.

He gave Mozza the thumbs up, then jerked both thumbs in the direction of their OP. Both men slid back down the slope they had been lying on, put their PNGs back on, and started for home across the patchwork of hummocks and hollows, Mozza in the lead.

They had gone hardly 100 yards when a quietly spoken fragment of Spanish seemed to rise out of the silence, like a record fade-out in reverse. At almost the same instant a figure appeared above them, a blue silhouette against the night clouds, not more than 10 feet away.

Stanley's Browning made a sound like a stuttering cough and as the figure began to collapse another appeared, like the second in a line of ducks in a fairground booth. Mozza sent three bullets into the shadowy mass of the man's trunk, and he folded with a sickening groan.

Silence reasserted itself. The two SAS men stood motionless, eyes and ears straining for sight or sound of other enemy soldiers. For a moment there was none, but a slight scraping noise beyond the two corpses betrayed the third Argentinian.

He could have run off into the dark or started shouting, but he ran straight over the rise towards them like a lunatic, waving his gun around in search of a target. The combined power of the two Brownings threw him backwards in a tangled heap.

'Christ almighty,' Mozza murmured.

Stanley was already working out what to do with the bodies. The only digging tools they had were their hands, and it would take longer than they had to bury three men in such a manner. But just leaving them where they were would invite discovery. Once they failed to report in, a search would be mounted, and before too long helicopter searchlights would be beaming down on the corpses.

'We'll have to cover them somehow,' he decided. 'With grass.' He pulled the three bodies down into the hollow while Mozza tore out clumps of tussock grass. Somehow they managed to weave the long grass around and between the dead men in such a way that the first gust of wind would not blow it away.

'Good enough,' Stanley said. 'Let's go.'

They regained the OP without further mishap, but one look at the two men's faces told Brookes that something had happened.

'Trouble,' Stanley told him. 'We ran into three

Argies. Could have been a regular patrol or maybe not – there was no way of knowing. But they were armed. We took them out and covered them up, but they'll be missed sooner or later.'

Brookes looked at Mozza. 'You OK?' he asked.

'Yeah,' Mozza said, nodding. It had all been so quick. He was not sure how he was.

'The kid was brilliant,' Stanley said.

'What now, boss?' Hedge asked.

Brookes looked at his watch. It was 1913 hours. He told the other three about the message from Hemmings, and what he had read between the lines.

'I think you're wrong about that, boss,' Hedge said. 'Hemmings didn't strike me as the sort of guy who'd go in for hints – he'd just say it straight out. But . . .'

'You may . . .' Brookes started to interrupt.

'But having said that,' Hedge went on inexorably, 'I still think it's a fucking good idea, no matter who had it.'

'It's got my vote,' Stanley agreed. 'If we stay here they'll keep looking till they find us. So, if we've got to go, then we might as well take in all the sights on our way home. Like those concrete shelters.'

'The landing's tomorrow,' Brookes argued. 'The fleet will be at its most vulnerable. It's the one day they can't afford to be surprised by those Super Es.'

'They can't be surprised by planes that we've already blown up,' Stanley said emphatically.

'I know,' Brookes agreed. 'But it's a risk nevertheless. If we fail . . .'

'Who dares wins, boss,' Hedge said straight-faced.

'OK. We're all agreed? Right. Next question – do we seek approval from the Green Slime?'

'The way I see it, boss,' Stanley said, 'is that we're the ones on the spot, and we're the ones who'll be playing beat the clock with the Argies out there. We know what's what. And we don't have time to fuck around with politics.'

'Agreed,' Hedge said. 'At least, mostly. But why not tell them what we're about to do, preferably just before we do it? If they agree, great. If they don't, we'll have to think up some reasons why we had to go ahead and do it anyway.'

Brookes smiled. 'Very pragmatic,' he said.

'That's me, boss,' Hedge agreed.

'OK,' Brookes said decisively. 'I've been thinking this over for a couple of days now, and there are certain obvious problems. First off, the subs are busy looking after the Task Force till the landing's over, so they can't come for us before Sunday at the earliest. Our only other escape route is across the Chilean border, which, as you all know, is about 40 miles the other side of the airbase. But we can't go rushing round the airbase with 90lb bergens on our backs, so we'll have to leave them somewhere for the duration. If we leave them this side of the base we'll have to work our way right round the place after all hell has broken loose, so it seems better to move everything across to the far side first. OK? Is that all clear?'

They all murmured assent, their faces deadly serious. Each of them was beginning to realize just how difficult getting away with it was going to be.

'So,' Brookes continued, 'we'll pack everything up and start off around nine, which will give us three hours to get round the base with all our kit, stash it somewhere, and be ready for a midnight start. Any questions?'

There were none. Or at least none of the sort Brookes intended.

'We could set up in competition with Pickfords,' Wacko muttered, as the patrol prepared for yet another move, this time back to the forward OP. It was two hours after nightfall.

The shower promised them by the Task Force's meteorological experts had lasted about seven hours, and showed no sign of giving way to one of the promised bright periods. 'It's going to be more like a swimming pool than a home,' Ben complained.

'A man's castle is his swimming pool,' Razor added helpfully.

'Keep it down, lads,' Docherty admonished them. He was beginning to worry that the sheer incompetence of the enemy's search that day had engendered a dangerous overconfidence.

'Sorry, boss,'

And then again, Docherty thought, he was probably overreacting. They had seen the Argentinians wend their way back into the base, and in any case the rain and wind were more than loud enough to drown out the sound of lowered voices. Even so, bad habits were catching.

He considered the latest fruit of Razor's new preoccupation with mixing proverbs – 'Don't cross a bridge with a stitched chicken' – and smiled to himself.

'We're ready, boss,' Ben whispered.

They started off down the hill, and Docherty had a last look back at the OP site before putting on his PNGs. From 10 feet away there was no sign it had ever existed. And until someone or something had the misfortune to fall through the turf roof there would not be.

It took them a couple of cautious hours to cover the two miles to the forward OP, and another hour to bale it out sufficiently for any sort of even vaguely comfortable occupation. At least the rain had stopped by the time they finished, and over the next two hours a sky of broken clouds gave way to a cold and welcome clarity.

Docherty reported their move back to Hemmings, and had the following morning's landing on East Falkland confirmed. Tomorrow, he thought, as he lay back in the theoretical pursuit of sleep, tomorrow a lot of kids who had never seen real action would find out something about themselves they had never known before. That their instinct for survival was stronger than they had thought, or, more frighteningly, that it was a lot weaker. That a grown man's bladder really did have a will of its own. That time was as elastic as any dope-smoker knew it was. That nothing could be as ugly as death. Or as peaceful.

The smell of the damp earth walls was heavy in his nostrils. It was a good smell, he decided. The smell of life. As he drifted into sleep he saw one last picture in his mind: the myriad floating candles on the moonlit Lake of Patzcuaro, a fragile flame for each and every ancestor on the Mexican Day of the Dead.

Raul was again late arriving at the Rakosi, and this time the long wait wore more heavily on Isabel, who looked up each time the door opened, hoping for Raul, but half-expecting Tomas Solanille. When Raul did finally appear he was with several of his fellow pilots, and already the worse for drink. He greeted her with a kiss and the usual smile, but she could immediately see that he was in a bad state.

It did not take long to find out the reason: the next day the English were probably going to land, and the Air Force was supposed to stop them. The Rakosi was full of pilots who thought so and said so, loudly. The Army would do nothing, the Navy would do nothing. Fucking eunuchs, every last one of them. The Air Force had to do it all. If it was not for them the nation would have no honour.

One man who claimed to have a son in the Navy, and who objected to the pilots' blanket condemnation of all things naval, was hurled out into the street.

Isabel managed to get Raul away from his companions, and into one of the booths. His aggressiveness vanished, and he became desperately maudlin. 'This will be our last meeting,' he said. The next day he would be killed, and he wanted her to write to Mariella, but not to sign her real name, because Mariella might not understand his knowing another woman, so it would be better if she signed herself Pablo, or something like that.

Eventually she managed to persuade him that his chances of survival on the next day would not be improved by dulling his reflexes with an excess of alcohol, and that she was hungry, and that there was a nice restaurant in Calle San Martín where she could eat and he could drink coffee.

He sheepishly agreed, and an hour later was *compos mentis* enough to provide the information she most wanted. She had seen Solanille again, she said.

'The friend of your family,' he remembered.

'Is he based here?' she asked. 'I would like to pay my respects.'

He was based in Rio Gallegos, Raul thought. And in the town, not at the airbase. He was something to do with Intelligence, so he was probably based at their HQ on Calle Zapiola, opposite the police station.

They went for their usual walk through the park by the river, though the conversation seemed more stilted than usual. She was thinking that maybe he was right, and that this would be the last time she would see him. He now seemed preoccupied with the day to come, almost eager to be on his way.

'Thanks for looking after me,' he said when they parted, throwing her one more sad smile as his taxi sped off back towards the airbase.

She walked down Avenida Julio Roca, past her hotel, and for another couple of blocks before turning left down Calle Ameghino. From the next corner she could see across Calle Zapiola to where several lights blazed in an elegant three-storey building. Maybe Solanille was in there now, writing his memoirs.

She turned and started walking back to the hotel, telling herself she was being foolish. The man had not laid a finger on her, turned any electric switches, forced her to eat her own shit, or raped her on a rack.

He had just sent her to those who had.

Shortly before 2100 hours Mozza encoded Brookes's message – BELIEVE DISCOVERY IMMINENT STOP RELOCATING TO CHILE STOP FIVE SUPER ETENDARDS EYEBALLED STOP WILL ATTEMPT DEMOLITION EN ROUTE STOP OUT – transmitted it by 'burst', and then closed down the PRC319's reception capability.

A few minutes later the four fully loaded men were making their way in single file across the dark and broken landscape, wearing PNGs, silenced MP5s at the ready. There had been no audible outcry from the airbase during the last few hours, no sign whatsoever that the three men now wearing grass shrouds had been missed. So far fate seemed to be smiling on the SAS.

The weather too was lending a hand, in the form of a cold, persistent drizzle. Besides reducing visibility, such conditions were likely to reduce the enemy's enthusiasm for setting foot outdoors. If it stayed like this, Brookes mused hopefully, they might even get away.

But first things first, he told himself. First we get the planes, then we start worrying about saving our own skins. Even all four of their lives would be a cheap price to pay for saving a ship.

He wondered, not for the first time, if having such thoughts merely demonstrated a propensity for stupid heroics. He knew that was what his wife would think, and probably his sons would come to think so too, once they had had all sense of honour knocked out of them by either business or university. What the hell. It still seemed real to him, and where else on earth could he go for judgement other than to his own conscience?

Behind him Mozza's watchful countenance also hid a turbulent state of mind. The killing of the Argentinian – the first man he had ever fired on in combat – had left him . . . well, it was hard to say. His senses seemed heightened, but that might have more to do with the danger they were all in. He also felt a dull ache in his stomach, but Hedge would say that was just hunger. Mozza did not know. He wanted a chance to think it all through, but it looked as though that would have to wait.

They were skirting the western end of the runway now, the nearest airbase buildings half a mile distant. Somewhere ahead of them was the main highway, and just as that thought came to Mozza the lights of a car appeared, and began working their way across the patrol's line of march.

They crossed a rough fence which seemed to separate a sheep meadow from airbase property, and five minutes later reached the road. They crossed close to a stream bridge, and followed the stream up a shallow, rock-strewn valley for a few minutes more before Brookes called a halt and indicated a particular tumble of rocks. 'This will do,' he whispered.

The drizzle had stopped. They removed what they would need and stashed the bergens in convenient crevices. Each would carry a silenced MP5 and Browning, but only two men were carrying anything on their backs: in Stanley's case a canvas bag packed with explosive devices; in Hedge's a lethal crossbow.

They moved back down the valley, crossed the highway and traversed the long stretch of rough grassland. As they neared the end of the long runway cloud-reflected light from the airbase allowed them to dispense with the PNGs.

The previous night they had failed to find any sign of an alarm mechanism in the wire fence, but Brookes still had his heart in his mouth as he bent down to begin cutting. He could hardly believe their security could be this lax.

But it was. A minute later they were all through the flap, and Brookes was doing his best to render the break invisible with wire clips. The runway stretched towards the distant cluster of faint lights, and the four men began advancing alongside it in single file. It was ten minutes to midnight.

They had gone barely 100 yards when the lights on either side winked on. For a moment Brookes thought they had been seen, but the sound of an approaching plane provided a more reassuring reason for the sudden illumination. The four men spread themselves out flat on the grass and waited.

The plane – a Pucara – roared past, its wheels touching down alarmingly near them, sending spray into the air. Almost instantly the runway lights were extinguished. At least someone was awake in the control tower, Brookes decided. It was not exactly a comforting thought.

He wondered whether to wait until the airbase's sudden burst of activity had died down, and decided not to. For all he knew a whole squadron of planes was on its way to Rio Grande.

The patrol resumed its progress, and after a few minutes the blaze of something like a camp-fire became visible in the vicinity of the concrete shelters. On West Falkland the Argentinian sentries had often hunkered down around such fires, and Brookes thought that was probably the case here. He hoped there would not be too many of them.

The patrol moved away from the side of the runway and veered out onto open ground, so as to give themselves a line of approach to the rear of the concrete shelters. As they approached the built-up part of the airbase the ambient light grew slightly stronger, to the point where the PNGs again became as much of a hindrance as a help. Brookes found it hard to understand the overall level of illumination;

it was as if one person had demanded a blackout for security against air attack, another had demanded bright lights as protection against a ground incursion, and the two of them had been forced to compromise on the sort of dim lighting that would have graced a Victorian street.

Still, he was not complaining. The first of the half-built concrete shelters was only 100 yards ahead, and there seemed nothing to prevent them rendering at least three of the Super Etendards incapable of inflicting any damage.

They reached the rear of the first completed shelter, and Brookes hand-signalled Stanley and Hedge to reconnoitre around either side. While Brookes and Mozza waited for them to return, the PC gently ripped several clumps of grass from the sandy soil, smoothed out the surface with his hand and etched out a plan of the three shelters. When the other two returned five minutes later they were able to fill in the exact placing of the fire and four sentries.

The fire was more or less midway between the first and second shelters, and almost level with an imaginary line drawn through their front walls. Three men were sitting around it. Stanley raised one finger and then put his hands together behind one ear to show that one of them was asleep. The fourth man was slowly pacing to and fro along the line of the three huts.

Brookes thought for a moment then indicated on the diagram what he expected from the others. They all nodded.

Stanley went down the side of the shelter furthest from the fire, while Mozza took off on a long semi-circular walk which would take him down between the second and third shelters, where he would be able to intercept anyone running towards the centre of the airbase. Brookes and Hedge waited by the corner of the space between the first and second, taking turns to keep the men around the fire under observation.

Five long minutes passed, and it was beginning to seem as if the walking sentry had stopped walking when Hedge saw him emerge from the other side of the second shelter, exchange some undecipherable pleasantry with his two conscious comrades, and disappear behind the front of the first shelter.

Stanley, concealed behind the far corner, listened to the sound of the Argentinian's boots on the gravel growing slowly more distinct. Then he could hear breathing, the sharp intake of someone dragging on a cigarette, and the man was there, not four feet away from him, a black shape against the grey night. As he turned Stanley stepped forward, one hand reaching round to cover the mouth, the other drawing the sharp blade across the bare throat.

There was rush of blood, a slight, almost inaudible gurgle. Stanley lowered the body carefully to the ground, removed the man's peaked cap, and placed it over his woolly hat. Then he picked the cigarette up from where it had fallen and started walking back towards the fire some 40 yards away.

Something in his walk must have been wrong, because one of the men by the fire suddenly looked up suspiciously. 'Sal?' he asked.

'*Si?*' Stanley said.

The man went for the rifle beside him, but his fingers were nowhere near the trigger when Stanley's Browning put a double tap through his upper torso.

His companion was quicker, ducking out of Stanley's

sight as he grabbed for his M16, but any sense of self-congratulation was laid to rest by the crossbow bolt which Hedge put through the back of his neck.

The third man, rudely awakened by the violent demise of the first, did not even bother to go for a weapon. He just launched himself out of his chair and into the possible salvation of the darkness. Stanley's Browning stopped him dead in his tracks.

The SAS men held their positions for a moment, ears straining for sounds of an enemy response.

There was none. Stanley and Hedge propped up the three Argentinians by the fire, and even added some broken packing cases to the flames. They did not exactly look real, but they would fool the eyes of any pilot coming in to land.

Brookes meanwhile was checking out the doors of the concrete shelter. His heart sank when he saw a state-of-the-art combination code plate beside it, but tried simply sliding the door anyway. It opened.

Inside his narrow-beam torch picked out the familiar nose-cone of the French-built jet. There was no sign of missiles, either Exocet or any other kind.

Stanley appeared beside him, the bag of explosives held loose in his right hand. 'How long, boss?' he asked softly, removing the time fuses and packets of C4 explosive.

'Say half an hour for this one. The same minus the time elapsed for the next, et cetera. OK? And keep it simple – just the nose-cones will do.'

He went back outside, hoping that half an hour would not be too long, or too short. They needed their presence to remain undetected at least long enough to find the other Super Etendards, and a few minutes extra for getting away would do no harm at all. On the other hand, if their presence was detected before the half hour was up then the enemy would have a chance to defuse the explosives.

There was no correct answer to this one – only the interplay of judgement and luck.

Stanley came out and they moved on to the second shelter, passing the three dead men around the fire. For some reason Brookes was reminded of the three trolls turned to stone in *The Hobbit*, a book he had often read to his boys when they were young. He had enjoyed them then, he thought, and maybe they had enjoyed it too.

Hedge had moved on up ahead, covering their front, while Mozza had been sent back to cover their rear. He took up station on the corner where Stanley had cut the guard's throat, his eyes drawn against his will to the pool of blood which had once sustained a life.

Stanley finished fixing the second plane, and Brookes waved Mozza up one shelter. Five minutes later all three fuses were burning, and the four men were gathered together in the shadow of the farthest shelter wall. Ahead of them a small parapet wall marked the perimeter of the large expanse of tarmac fronting the main hangars and, further on, the civilian airport building. There was precious little cover.

They had only twenty minutes before the explosives detonated, but there was always a chance no one would hear the small charges.

Two Aeromacchis were parked almost within spitting distance. 'Should we take them out?' Stanley asked.

'No,' Brookes said. 'At least not until we've made sure we've got all the Super Es.' There was no sign of any more guards, which did not mean there were none.

Once the four of them moved out of the shadows they might be visible from the control tower away to the left, but at least it was lit within, which would make it difficult for anyone inside to see out.

The fuses were burning away. 'OK,' Brookes decided, 'let's take the hangars one by one.'

He led off at a canter, swinging across the parapet wall, and the others followed. For the first time they were out in the light, and it felt like it.

They reached the first hangar door, and Hedge started sliding open a large enough gap for them to enter by. There was a harsh screeching sound of unoiled wheels, which seemed to hang in the damp night air. They all froze, but there was no indication anyone else had heard it.

The hangar contained several Pucaras, and Brookes shook his head to Stanley's gestured enquiry.

They moved on to the next, where Hedge took his time with the door, and managed to ease it sideways in virtual silence. Brookes was just squeezing through the crack when a voice rang out in the distance.

'Control tower,' Mozza whispered. 'He wants to know if we're "Díaz".'

'Díaz has changed shifts,' Brookes shouted back in Spanish. He could see a figure standing at the top of the control tower steps, a cigarette glowing as he took a drag.

'Who are you?' the man wanted to know.

'Gómez,' Brookes shouted back, raising his MP5. As the man backed through the doorway both he and Stanley opened fire with their silenced SMGs. The man seemed to leap from sight, and the sound of glass breaking carried across the intervening space.

Please be alone, Brookes pleaded, and for a few

seconds an unbroken stillness and silence seemed to answer his prayer. Then the light in the control tower abruptly went out, and the sound of a swelling air-raid siren filled the air.

For a few seconds they seemed paralysed by the sound.

'Any ideas, boss?' Hedge asked.

Brookes awoke from his momentary trance. 'Let's keep moving,' he said. 'Stanley, take the front. Mozza, Tail-end Charlie.' In the distance they could all hear motors revving.

They ran forward along the front of a third hangar, and Brookes looked inside as the others listened to the growing tumult of the enemy's awakening. Brookes was just re-emerging when a jeep loaded with men careered round the far corner of the building. Stanley and Hedge opened fire, sending the vehicle spinning out of control and into the corrugated hangar wall with a sound like a giant gong being struck.

No one emerged from the wreckage.

Stanley walked forward, and then ducked back quickly as someone opened up in his direction with an automatic rifle. He took cover behind a fork-lift truck loaded with empty pallets.

The PC looked at his watch, and turned to Hedge and Mozza. 'Hedge, get behind the parapet. Mozza, get back towards the shelters in case they try and outflank us. We'll be joining you shortly.'

He took cover himself behind the tailplane of a parked Aeromacchi, conscious of enemy movement on the tarmac ahead of them. 'We have to hold them for three minutes,' he shouted to Stanley.

'Piece of cake,' the Brummie shouted back. 'By the way,' he added almost conversationally, 'there's another couple of Super Es just round the corner there. I'd just seen 'em when the bastards opened fire.'

'I think they'll probably object if we walk over and plant some plastic on their noses,' Brookes observed. He fired a burst with his MP5, and there was a crash of someone diving, or falling, back behind cover.

'If I can get behind that truck,' Stanley shouted, indicating the fuelling tanker to his left, I can at least put a few holes in them.'

'Wait till we hear the others have gone up,' he ordered, and checked his watch. They should have blown by now.

He looked back just in time to see a flicker of light and to hear the first of the slight whooshing sounds he was waiting for. That was one Super Etendard which would not be launching an Exocet against a British ship. And that was another. And another.

Three down, two to go. He could see Argentinian troops moving up on the far side of the runway, and knew that there was no way they were going to get away from the airbase. They might as well do all the damage they possibly could.

'I'll cover you,' he shouted, knowing full well – and knowing that Stanley knew full well – that any covering fire he could provide in this situation was about as useful as a paper umbrella. Still, he began spraying three bursts in a random pattern across the entire front.

Stanley catapulted out from behind the fork-lift, took seven or eight running paces and launched himself into the roll which would take him behind the truck. As he disappeared from Brookes's sight the truck exploded in a huge sheet of flame, hit by Argentinian fire. Brookes bowed his head, blinding lights dancing on his retinas. Then, seduced by the sudden thought that everyone would be equally blinded, he launched himself in a slalom-like run across the tarmac, his MP5 waiting for its target.

Ten paces, twenty, and there was the nose-cone . . .

A violent pain in his chest seemed to come from nowhere, to well up and engulf him, and the lights went out.

Hedge saw him go down. He knew Brookes and Stanley must have had some good reason for doing impersonations of the Charge of the Light Brigade, but whether he would ever find out what it was seemed open to question. Still, he had to try.

He eased himself across the parapet with the intention of advancing in a crouching run. He had hardly gone two paces when the burst of fire hit him, and knocked him down like a skittle. With a supreme effort, and the good fortune of some poor enemy shooting, he managed to lever himself back across the wall.

Neither Brookes nor Stanley had moved out on the tarmac, and there seemed to be a lot of troops milling around beyond them. Hedge took as good a look at his wounds as he could manage in the dim light. It seemed like one bullet had shattered the shinbone, another had pierced the knee. He would not be going anywhere under his own steam for quite a while. It also hurt like hell.

He tried to lever himself up onto one leg, and sank back with a grimace of pain. He exhaled noisily and examined the darkness behind him, just in time to see Mozza materialize out of it. 'They haven't got round behind us yet,' Mozza said. 'Let's . . .' His voice trailed off as he saw the body of Brookes stretched out on the distant tarmac. And failed to locate the fourth member of the patrol. 'Where's Stanley?' he asked.

'Somewhere under that truck,' Hedge said brutally. 'And . . .'

'Is the boss dead?'

'Dunno. But it doesn't look like he's going anywhere, and neither am I, so you get the fuck out of here, Mozza, while you still can.'

'I'm not deserting you,' Mozza insisted. He listened for sounds of pursuit but could hear none.

'The hell you aren't,' Hedge said, grabbing Mozza's sleeve. 'Listen to me, you numbskull,' he hissed. 'We've sent a few Argies to meet their maker here, and their mates are not going to be very pleased. Plus, we're not wearing uniforms and they're going to think they don't need any more excuse. And if they get all of us then there's no witnesses, right? They can do what they want, and when the time comes make up some cock-and-bull story about us all being killed in battle or lost at sea. But if you get away then the rest of us have got a chance of getting out of this alive. Got it?

'Yeah, I . . .'

'Then fucking go!'

Mozza went.

Ten rapid strides took him behind the hangar, and hopefully out of sight of the enemy. In the darkness he stopped to put on the PNGs, took a deep breath, and told his feet to be still while he spent ten precious seconds of running time in coherent thought.

There was no hope of retracing the patrol's entry route along the runway – that direction would take him back into the light, and back into the arms of the Argies. His best bet was to head in the general direction of the road, and hope he could find some way under, over or through the fence without any cutting equipment.

He moved off at a run, along the back of the hangar, and across an open stretch of darkened ground between a stagnant-looking lagoon and several lighted barracks. No shouts pursued him — only the distant sound of gunfire: Hedge must be still drawing fire and holding up the advance.

As the thought crossed his mind the gunfire stopped. Mozza hoped to God it had stopped because Hedge had surrendered.

He veered round the end of a darkened building and into another stretch of open ground. A hundred yards in front of him the airbase entry-exit road passed through a wide gateway in the fence and onto the highway beyond. One floodlight stood above the security checkpoint.

The idea of using stealth to escape flickered across his mind, but failed to take a hold. He was too wired up, too psyched out by the events of the last fifteen minutes, to even consider slowing down. Still running, he aimed himself at the open gateway like a torpedo, and for reasons he could not begin to understand, found himself wailing like a banshee as he did so.

A guard emerged from the doorway, more surprised than ready, and Mozza's MP5 took out both him and his companion before they could fire a shot. If he had not seen the two motorbikes leaning against the far wall he would probably have kept running straight across the highway and on towards the centre of the island.

But somehow the bikes registered in his consciousness, and brought him to a halt. He looked back —

no one was heading his way, not yet at least. The bikes were both 250cc Yamahas, and of a type he had ridden before, both in Hereford and Manchester. He got astride one, rolled it a few feet and then fired two treble-tap bursts into the tyres of the other, before throwing the MP5 into the darkness.

He rolled his machine out onto the highway, which sloped down towards the south, away from the direction he wanted to go. Or did he? He forced himself to spend time thinking it through. The way back to their kit was to the right, but what was there in his pack that he needed? There was no way anyone from the Task Force was going to come and collect him, so the radio would be no help.

What the hell – a silent exit was the best start of all, and the best thing he could do was get as far away from the airbase as fast as he could, in any direction. Once he was far enough away he could start heading west towards Chile. He eased the Yamaha onto the slope, and freewheeled away from the airbase gates. The hill went on and on, as if placed there by a friendly god, and he was almost a quarter of a mile from the gates before he needed to slip the bike into gear. The noise seemed deafening, but there was no sign of chasing lights on the road behind him.

He tried to picture the detailed map which Brookes had been carrying. Almost opposite the airbase, he seemed to remember, there was a turn-off which ran in a roughly westerly direction all the way to the border.

He had no sooner had the thought than a turn-off appeared. It had to be the one. Mozza swerved off the highway and onto the gravelled track, slowing down until he was more sure of the surface. It was OK, he decided. At a steady 30 miles per hour he could be at the border in an hour. But first . . .

He brought the bike to a halt, took out his Browning and used the butt to smash both front and rear lights. Then he replaced the PNGs and started off again. The track ran across the same sort of landscape they had first encountered after landing on the island: not exactly flat, but gently undulating grassland with little vegetation above knee height, just a few stunted trees in the stream bottoms. It was an easy ride, Mozza thought, but as the miles passed he began to get the distinct impression that the road was curving more and more to the south, and away from his intended direction.

The illuminated compass said he was going south-westwards, but compasses were notoriously unreliable this near to the poles. Meanwhile the sky was showing signs of clearing. It was not, he thought, as if he had any real choice but to follow this road wherever it went. Not when the alternative was a return to the airbase.

When the sky cleared he could get a proper fix from the stars. He resumed his journey across the dark and apparently empty landscape, and soon the road turned comfortingly towards the west. It held this direction for several miles, descending gentle rises to ford shallow streams and climbing gentle rises to begin descending again. It was like crossing a vast, wrinkled face.

Stars were becoming visible between the clouds as the road took another wide turn towards what he thought was the south. Another fifteen minutes and the clear sky to the south confirmed Mozza's worst fears. He was not on the road he wanted to be on.

He came to a halt and took off the PNGs. Almost directly ahead of him the four stars of the Southern Cross hung in the heavens. Extend the longer arm by four and half times its length, he told himself, and from that point draw a line vertically to the ground. That was the way to the South Pole. And he was heading directly towards it.

He let his mind wander for a moment, enjoying the unfolding majesty of the night sky: the inky depth of the Coal Sack hard by the Southern Cross, the yellow-white brilliance of Canopus low to the right, the almost devilish red glow of Antares above and to his left, like Sauron's eye in *Lord of the Rings*. The whole Milky Way seemed to float like a huge veil across space.

Faced with all that, the direction of the road seemed somehow less important. Unless and until it made a definitive turn to the east, Mozza decided, he would stay with it as long as he could. It was now approaching two o'clock, and in about four hours he would need to be under cover.

The road now seemed set in its ways, rarely deviating from its southward course. It was also climbing steadily, and the landscape was losing its openness, with stretches of grassland first alternating with swathes of trees, then giving way altogether to a rapidly thickening forest. It was in a rare break from the trees that Mozza noticed the first major signs of human occupancy he had seen since leaving the highway: a group of buildings clustered in the shelter of a valley away and down to his right. He wondered what they would make of the sound of his bike, and whether they would do anything about such an unexpected intrusion. There would be no telephone out here, but whoever it was might well be in radio contact with civilization.

There was nothing he could do about it if they were. He rode on, out of the forest and onto another stretch of high moorland, before the track came to an abrupt and unexpected end by the side of a rushing stream. The remains of a house, apparently long consumed by fire, sat on an adjacent rise.

Mozza concealed the Yamaha in a cluster of bushes that overhung the stream, took his bearings from the heavens, and headed out along the bank of the stream towards its source. Away to the west across the open heath, anything from 10 to 40 miles away, lay the Chilean border, but he now knew there was no chance of reaching it by dawn. Given that, he wanted tree cover by the time the sun came up, and memory told him the further south he went the more chance he had of finding it.

He knew he was physically tired, but adrenalin was still pumping life into his limbs, and he managed a steady four miles an hour across the often spongy surface. There was still an hour of darkness left when he found himself entering the fringe of a beech forest. Another half a mile brought him to what looked an ideal spot for a shelter. The earth-choked roots of a fallen tree offered a windbreak, and with some judicious scraping out and covering of gaps he had a relatively cosy, hard-to-detect place to sleep.

The thought of a cup of tea was almost irresistible, but he knew a fire would be too great a risk. Instead he breakfasted on water and a biscuit, and stretched himself out to sleep in the shelter he and nature had made together. Through the gaps in his roof he could see the fading stars, but now that he was motionless their stillness seemed almost depressing, like a reminder of his aloneness in the universe.

He remembered a psychological technique Lynsey had told him about – 'visualization' it was called, and that was what it was. You just had to visualize things you wanted as a way of making it more likely that they would come true. At least that was how he remembered her description of it.

He closed his eyes and tried to visualize his home-coming: Lynsey opening the door of the flat and the smile on her face as she opened her arms to take him in.

8

Soon after first light on that same morning a young Argentinian lieutenant was the first unfriendly witness to the British landing in San Carlos Water. He radioed his army superiors in Port Stanley that two landing craft were discharging troops. But since Argentinian experts had already declared San Carlos an impossible spot for the landing the lieutenant's superiors could only believe he must be imagining things.

The Argentinian Navy had intercepted the signal, however, and thought it worthwhile sending an Aeromacchi to check out the story. Its pilot flew blithely across the last ridge before San Carlos Water and was more than a little shocked to find what appeared to be the entire British fleet spread out before him. Less surprisingly, he beat a hasty retreat.

On the ships themselves, and in the defensive positions busily being constructed ashore, the British spent the next hour or so casting anxious eyes at the clear blue skies overhead. When would the enemy Air Force put in its first appearance *en masse*?

On the hill to the south of Rio Gallegos, Docherty and Ben watched the Mirages take to the air, arc away across the city and fade into the sky

197

above the ocean. 'SEVEN MIRAGES DEPART RIO GALLEGOS 0842', Ben typed onto the keypad.

Ten minutes later four Skyhawks took to the air, and followed the same path out towards the Task Force, some 400 miles to the east in San Carlos Water and Falkland Sound. Ben's two typing fingers recorded the departure, and from the *Resource* it was relayed to the Task Force operational centre, and from there to the Sea Harriers hovering above the approaches to the islands.

On board the *Resource* Hemmings experienced a variety of emotions as the morning wore on. North was providing all the advanced warning that could have been expected, but the Mirages and Skyhawks were dropping to sea level before attacking, and there was still little the Sea Harriers could do to intercept them on their way in. At least the Task Force knew that no Super Etendards had left Rio Gallegos airbase that morning, and that there would be no surprise Exocet attack from that direction. North could have done no more.

As for South, there had been no news of any kind since the cryptic message the previous night, which Hemmings had received with a rare mixture of admiration and anger. The 'take-it-or-leave-it-but-we-know-best' style seemed to exemplify both the finest traditions of the SAS and irresponsibility on a grand scale. Where the hell were the four men now? Had they managed to put the Super Etendards out of action? There had been no reports of the plane that morning, which gave Hemmings grounds for hope, but there had been no radio contact from the patrol either, which gave him cause for anxiety.

And not just for the four men under Brookes's

command. If any of them had been captured, who knew what sort of treatment they were receiving from the enemy. The Argentinian military hardly inspired confidence, and the fact that the SAS men were out of uniform – thanks to the bloody politicians in London – would not exactly help their case. If things got nasty . . .

The SAS men were trained to withstand certain interrogation techniques, but not many men could hold out against the sort of brutality some regimes practised. And if any of them broke, then both Docherty's patrol and the woman in Rio Gallegos were in danger.

Hemmings cursed himself for giving her name to South, and wondered how long he could afford to wait before warning North. They could nothing before nightfall in any case. So why distract them from the important job they were doing? He wished he could send a submarine to pick North up, but all of them were needed to protect the Task Force from their Argentinian counterparts for as long as the landing operation required.

Hedge guessed it was sometime in the late morning, but he had no way of knowing for sure. The small room they had placed him in had no windows, and his watch had been removed by one of the soldiers. What was more, he seemed to have been slipping in and out of either sleep or unconsciousness ever since they had carried him in from where he had fallen.

They had not been gentle. Either the destruction of the three Super Es or the death of their comrades – maybe both – had enraged the Argie troops, and no effort had been made to spare him any pain as they manhandled him across the airbase towards his current lodgings in this anonymous room. Hedge reckoned he could not blame them: he knew how pissed off he would have been if the boot had been on the other foot.

Since then, however, he had mostly been left alone. On the only occasion he had been visited, by two officers in Air Force uniform, Hedge had feigned both an inability to understand Spanish and virtual unconsciousness, confining himself to an array of moans which he hoped would produce some medical attention. He had already reached his own diagnosis: the injury to his calf, while painful, was not serious, but the knee was in really bad shape. Such bad shape, in fact, that he was trying not to think about the possible implications for his future life. Always assuming he had one.

A man had eventually arrived with hot water and bandages, and, whether or not he was a doctor, had proved to possess remarkably gentle hands. Unfortunately he had not left any painkillers behind. Or any food.

Hedge would have liked to start banging on the door and demanding tortillas, or whatever it was they ate in Tierra del Fuego, but standard practice in such situations dictated a more restrained form of behaviour. He was supposed to pretend to be more tired and more badly injured than he was, just in case the Argies took it into their heads to start asking him questions with the gloves off. No torturer liked his victim to be continually slipping into unconsciousness.

Hedge shivered, and hoped he would be able to cope if and when the time came. He wondered where

Mozza was. For all he knew, the boy was in the room next door. Come to that, he was not even sure that Brookes and Stanley were dead.

There was the sound of a key in the lock. Hedge lay there with his eyes shut and feigned sleep.

'I think you are awake, Englishman. And I think you probably speak Spanish as well. My name is Segrera, Colonel Segrera of the Argentinian Air Force. I am here to inform you that Military Intelligence will soon be assuming responsibility for you. Before that happens – as one military man to another – would you like to ask me any questions?'

Hedge considered. The man sounded genuine. He opened his eyes and looked up at a thin-faced man with cropped, iron-grey hair. 'Are my companions dead?' he asked.

'Two of them are. The third escaped.'

Hedge's heart leapt, but his faced showed no sign of it.

'Will I be receiving any medical attention?' he asked.

'That will be up to Military Intelligence. There are no facilities here on the base.'

'And just exactly who are Military Intelligence?' Hedge asked, not really expecting an answer.

'My country's darker side,' the officer replied. 'If I were you, I would deal with them as carefully as you can.'

The sun was still high in the northern sky when Mozza woke. He did a 180-degree sweep of the surrounding countryside, and found only dappled forest in every direction. Feeling stiff, he scrambled out of the tree roots and tried some exercises. The pins and needles in his feet did not go away though, and removing his boots and socks he discovered a distinctly purple tinge to the skin, swelling and blisters. The trench foot which had threatened on West Falkland had finally come home to roost.

He felt a twinge of panic and let his mind settle back into reason. The only cure for trench foot was a combination of rest and warmth, and since he would have precious little of either until he reached Chile, there was not much point in getting himself in a state about it.

It was time to do some strategic thinking, he told himself sternly. First, he needed a good directional fix. Taking his knife he cut a three-foot length of straight branch from the nearest beech tree, and walked towards an area that looked light enough to be a clearing. Once in the sunlight, he pushed one end of the branch into the peaty ground and inserted a small twig where the shadow of the branch ended.

Back at the scrape he did an inventory of what he was carrying. He had two days' worth of high-calorie emergency rations in his escape belt, along with fish hooks and line, needle and cotton, and waterproof matches. The water bottle was still more than half full, and there was half a bar of chocolate in his jacket pocket. He was, he decided, unlikely to starve. And by the next morning, if he remained free, he should be far enough away to risk a fire and eat a decent hot meal.

In matters of clothing he was less well off. The Gore-tex jacket and trousers were warm enough for sea level, but from what he could remember the going would get higher before it got lower again. He was not really equipped for travelling in the snow, particularly at night.

He would worry about that when the time came. His only other serious problem – potentially, at least – was the state of his feet. And they would be warmer in motion than standing still. He gathered his stuff together and walked back to the sunlit clearing. Fifteen minutes had passed, and the shadow had moved significantly to the east. He placed another twig where it ended, removed the branch and used it to draw a line connecting the two twigs. He then checked his compass against this east-west axis, and found with much relief that it was hardly out at all. Now he could navigate with confidence at night whether or not the stars were visible.

Reckoning he had four hours before nightfall, Mozza started walking, keeping as close to a westerly direction as the configuration of the land would let him. At first the forest restricted his vision to not much more than 100 yards, but as the ground rose the trees became sparser, and a distant range of snow-capped mountains became increasingly visible. Eventually he emerged onto a small, bare plateau and found to his surprise that the range was a lot nearer than it looked: the snowy peaks had fooled him into thinking the mountains were bigger and further away. He was in fact confronting a range of snow-capped hills, and the snowline was only a few hundred yards above him.

For the next few miles the walking was ideal. He was on a north-facing slope – the warmer slope in the southern hemisphere – and out in the open, just above the tree line. Only once did the distant sound of a helicopter cause him to duck back beneath the cover of the trees, and that soon faded. It would not be the Argies who stopped him reaching Chile, Mozza decided. This was going to be a contest between himself and nature.

For the last hour of daylight he pushed against his own weariness, but it was only when he began to feel that his concentration was wandering that he decided to call a halt. The range of hills was behind him by this time, and he was back in the forest, working his way down a valley which seemed untouched by human presence. Animal tracks proliferated, particularly at stream-crossing points, and Mozza began to regret not bothering to enquire about the local predators before setting foot on Tierra del Fuego.

He made camp up against a north-facing, wind-sheltered cliff, and gathered wood for a fire as the dusk deepened. Not surprisingly, his feet were more swollen than before, and badly needed some real warmth. Without it, Mozza doubted if they would stand up to another whole day's walking. He had to risk a fire. The flames would only be visible from the south, and even if they were, there was nowhere for troops to be put down from a helicopter. He struck the match, applied it to the kindling, and warmed his feet by the growing flames as he ate two squares of chocolate.

The next requirement was a cooking utensil, and the only possible source was the forest. Mozza checked the trees around him, and settled on a species he did not recognize but which seemed close to birch in the texture of its bark. Using knife and fingers, he carefully stripped off a piece large enough for the cutting of a circle. Having laboriously removed the outer layer he folded the inner layer into four, fashioned a cone-shaped cup from it, and fastened it with several stitches of thick cotton.

Next he cut a long sapling and a forked twig, and balanced the former on the latter, so that one end could be weighted down by rocks and the other end used to suspend the cone cup over the fire. A sachet of dried soup was mixed with water and hung up to boil, with Mozza watching over the potentially combustible cone as his feet gently toasted. It all bought back memories of camping out with his brothers and sisters in the Peak District.

Once it was cooked he took his time drinking the soup, relishing each hot sip until it was all gone. He then boiled some water in the cone for tea, which he made with sachets of powdered tea, sugar and powdered milk. There were biscuits and another square of chocolate for dessert.

He had rarely tasted a better meal, Mozza thought. Only the special meal Lynsey had cooked him for his last birthday came to mind. He raised his cone of tea in a toast to her. 'I love her,' he told the forest. And I'm going to make it back to her, he told himself.

Four hundred miles or so to the east the British Army now had 4000 men ashore in the San Carlos beach head, and there was no sign of any significant response from those units of the Argentinian Army which were based in the islands. The same could not be said of the enemy air force, which had pressed home its attacks on the supporting fleet throughout the day with a great deal of skill and bravery. One frigate had been sunk, four others badly damaged, and it seemed mostly a matter of luck that the vital supply ships had emerged virtually unscathed.

The battle might be far from over, Hemmings thought to himself on the *Resource*, but the worst most probably was. The failure of the Super Etendards to put in an appearance might well have been crucial to the British success, and Hemmings hoped he knew the reason for their absence. But it was still proving impossible to raise South on the radio, and the patrol had not reported in. No matter what had gone right the night before, Hemmings had to assume something else had gone badly wrong in the meantime.

North should be told, that he was sure of. And Docherty's men should get themselves out of Argentina. Now that the troops were ashore, and now that they knew the Super Etendards were based at Rio Grande, any more information North could provide was hardly worth the risk, either to the men themselves or to Britain's diplomatic situation.

But what about the woman? Should he leave that to them? They were the ones who would be putting their lives at risk to warn her. Or was that unfair to her, leaving her fate in the hands of four men she had never met? Did she not deserve better of the British?

It was an impossible decision. The only comfort Hemmings could derive from the situation – and pretty cold comfort at that – lay in his inability to offer the SAS patrol any assistance in leaving Argentina. He would not order them to warn the woman, but he would suggest that she might be in a position to help them get away.

Docherty received the message with the sort of sinking feeling in his stomach he usually reserved for England-Scotland games at Hampden Park. Suddenly the lights of Rio Gallegos looked a lot further away than they had.

He showed the stored message to Ben, who rolled his

eyes heavenwards. 'Better wake the others,' Docherty whispered. He rubbed his eyes and tried to think the thing through. They were only about 30 miles from the Chilean border, the crossing of which was unlikely to present any problems. He could not imagine it was marked by more than a token fence, if that.

If they set out now there was at least an even chance they could make it before dawn.

Rio Gallegos, though, was in the opposite direction. If they wanted to warn the woman, then at least one of them could count on another fun-packed day in sunny Argentina.

'What's up, Doc?' Razor asked with a yawn.

Ben allowed him and Wacko to read the message for themselves.

'So we're on our way?' Wacko asked.

'That's what we have to decide,' Docherty said curtly.

'Which way?' Razor wanted to know.

'The quickest way out of this country is due south,' Docherty said. 'The border's about 30 miles away.'

'So what are we waiting for?' Wacko demanded. 'If we get a move on maybe we'll see some action on the Falklands.'

'If you'd read the message properly,' Docherty told him, 'you'd have seen that we're expected to camp out in Chile for as long as possible, so as not to embarrass anyone. And if the Chileans find us we'll probably be interned. Or at best flown back to England.'

Wacko shrugged. 'Still beats sleeping in a wet hole in Argentina.'

'The Cup Final's tomorrow,' Razor said wistfully.

'What about the woman?' Ben asked quietly.

'You're not serious!' Wacko exclaimed.

'She's fighting the same war, on the same side,' Ben argued. 'I think we should at least think about it.'

'OK,' Wacko said. 'This is what I think. She's an Argie communist. She's fighting her own war against her government and we just happen to be fighting them too. So she gets our help. She's just using us.'

Docherty tried to read Wacko's face in the gloom. There was some sense to what the man said, but there was a depth of anger accompanying the words which seemed out of all proportion to the subject. Did the mere *idea* of the woman make him angry?

'She's using us, we're using her,' Razor said. 'What's the difference? If she's on our side then we owe her.'

'Jesus Christ!' Wacko exploded.

'We don't all have to go into town,' Ben said. 'Maybe two of us, maybe only one. The others can start heading south. I'd volunteer to go in alone,' he said, 'but I'm the only one doesn't speak Spanish. But I'll go in with someone else.'

'I'll come along for the ride,' Razor said. 'Time waits for an old fool,' he added wisely.

They all started giggling, even Wacko. Somehow the knowledge that they were half-buried on a Patagonian hill doubled the absurdity of just about everything.

Docherty eventually brought them back to a semblance of order. 'I'm sorry to disappoint you, lads,' he said, 'but Ben here has the sort of ripe golden hair they don't often see in these parts, and Razor might as well have London tattooed on his forehead. I . . .'

'You, on the other hand, could be taken for Galtieri's father,' Razor said.

'Precisely,' replied Docherty. 'And I think it's a one-man job. You lot can head for Chile.'

'No way, boss,' Ben said. 'We'll wait for you here.'

'Yeah,' Wacko agreed, 'all for one and one for all and all that crap.'

'We'd be lost without you, boss,' Razor added. 'Where are we anyway?' he asked, looking round.

'I'm touched' Docherty said. 'But if I'm not back by morning . . .'

'We can assume she's beautiful, and you've decided to keep her all for yourself.'

'Something like that. Ben, let Hemmings know what's going on. I'm going to slip into something more comfortable, or at least less damp . . .'

'Not one of those Tartan condoms, boss?' Razor asked.

'Hey,' Ben said, 'that's not a bad idea. You could do them in all the various clan colours and sell them to the tourists.' He tried in vain to imagine Morag selling them in the shop. Still, the thought of her brought a pang to his heart, not to mention his loins. She had always had a wonderful way with her when it came to putting a condom on him.

Docherty re-emerged, if that was the right word for the squirming motion necessary to free him from the hide, and joined the three men squatting in the dark on the vast open hillside. He had exchanged the camouflage trousers for plain – the Green Slime had been unable to work out which would suit the colours of the steppe better – and was wearing them outside his boots, but otherwise his outfit was the same: Gore-tex jacket over thick sweater. The most striking change was to his face, which was free of 'cam' cream for the first time in five days.

He checked the action on the Browning High Power

and replaced it in his jacket pocket, then tied the cream's temporary replacement – a dark piece of cloth – around his face below the eyes.

'OK,' he whispered. 'I'll see you later. And keep down the noise,' he added over his shoulder.

'Good luck, boss,' Ben said softly.

'See if you can pick up any Spurs news, boss,' was Razor's parting shot.

It was slightly over four miles, Docherty reckoned, from the OP to the centre of Rio Gallegos. It would take about half an hour to reach the nearest road, then another hour into town, assuming he did not run into trouble on the way.

Somehow the prospect did not worry him. In fact, during his PNG-assisted passage across the dark and undulating landscape he felt an almost reckless sense of freedom. He was alone, in motion, imbued with purpose. Every sound seem magnified in the green world of the PNGs, and the feel of the breeze on his face seemed almost like a caress.

He reached the expected road, and started down a long slope. The lights of the airbase had disappeared from sight behind the hills to his left, but those of the town lay directly ahead.

Two cars passed him going in the opposite direction, and on both occasions he took care to dart out of sight as they approached. When one came up from behind him he considered hitching a lift, but swiftly dismissed the idea. His Spanish would pass muster, but he had no convincing cover story for being on this road.

The car swept past as he merged his shadow with that of a stunted tree by the roadside, and he watched its headlights illuminate the road into town. Another forty minutes of fast walking brought him to the outskirts, where new industrial developments were pushing untidily out into the grassy steppe. A wide avenue, which boasted the first happy-looking trees he had seen since Oxfordshire, led towards the town centre and the estuary. It seemed almost deserted of either traffic or pedestrians, but there were many lights on in the houses to either side.

He walked by some pedestrians: an arm-in-arm couple who did not even give him a first glance, let alone a second; then a youngish woman who did give him one swift look, but did not bother to repeat the experience. Docherty decided he could not look that unusual.

He walked down Calle Salta to the brightly lit Avenida Julio Roca, on which he knew the hotel was located. Here there was life: couples strolling along, cafés and restaurants doing business, groups of raucous young men hanging around on streets corners. He knew it should not, but somehow the normality of it all surprised him, maybe even upset him a little. This country was at war, but no one would have known it.

He supposed it was the same back home. The war would be on the news, and every evening the British people would be getting a vicarious dose of it. The rest of the time they would be going about their daily business, just like the people of Rio Gallegos. Tomorrow they would be watching the Cup Final and wondering whether it was Jimmy Hill's chin or beard which was that strange shape. And then going down the pub.

Docherty could see the neon sign for the Covadonga

Hotel not far ahead. He crossed over to the opposite pavement and bought a newspaper from a street vendor, thinking it might make him look marginally more like a member of the community. The vendor complained about the need to change a note, but seemed to find nothing surprising in Docherty's appearance.

He walked slowly on, studying the immediate vicinity of the hotel over the edge of the newspaper. There was no sign of police activity, no suspicious-looking characters leaning against walls or pretending to read newspapers. Other than himself, that was.

If she was at home, then he could tell her in person. But what if she was out? He supposed he could leave her a message – something she would understand but no one else would. But he would have to leave it with someone. Who would he say he was? What would fit in with her cover?

Isabel sat in the Renault, its window open to let in the breeze flowing over the estuary. Darkness had long since fallen, but she felt unable to drag herself away from the peace of the ruffled waters and star-strewn heavens.

All through the daylight hours her thoughts had been with the pilots contesting the skies over the Malvinas. Which, she had to admit, was pretty perverse. And not very helpful either, to them or herself.

The war could have been lost that morning, for all she knew. Certainly the Junta would be in no rush to publicize the end result of their own gross miscalculations. But even if it was still in full swing, the end could not be long delayed. She should be thinking about what to do when the time finally came.

Did she want to go back to England? It was a decent enough place to live, but ... She knew she could not just walk away from Argentina again. Here was where it had happened, and here was where it had to be exorcized, if such a thing was possible. She doubted that it was, but if she was ever to be truly alive again, then she had to try.

But how to begin? She could kill Solanille, she thought. It would not be difficult. If she did not care what happened to herself then she could do almost anything. But that would hardly be exorcism – just a potent cocktail of revenge and suicide.

She needed a drink, she decided, and there was a bottle of whisky in her hotel room. 'Fuck that for a game of soldiers,' she murmured in English. It had been one of Michael's favourite phrases, and only conceivable in a country where soldiers really did spend most of their time playing games.

No, she decided, she did not want to be alone. She turned the car round and drove across town to the Rakosi. It was almost empty, so she took a seat at the bar, where the barman-owner, Miguel, was catching up with his accounts. He looked depressed, but that was nothing unusual: his wife spent most evenings flirting with his customers.

He poured her a double whisky and said he thought he would have one himself. 'Problems?' she asked, almost eagerly. At least someone else's would be easier to cope with than her own.

'For all of us,' he said cryptically. 'I just got some news,' he added. 'The guy who delivers for the local brewery, well, he also does the airbase, and he'd just come from there.' He looked up and down the bar, as if anxious that no one else should hear. 'They lost seventeen planes today,' he said. '*Seventeen*,' he repeated, as if he could scarcely believe it himself.

'That's terrible,' she managed to say. Had Raul been one of them? She might never know. And what did it matter, she asked herself. If he was not, then someone else was.

Docherty walked confidently in through the front door of the Covadonga Hotel, and up to the reception desk, where Manuel Menéndez was poised over a crossword, chewing the end of his ballpoint pen.

'I would like to see Isabel Rodríguez,' Docherty told him.

Menéndez looked up at him hopefully. 'A cathedral town in France – eight letters?'

'Chartres,' Docherty told him. 'C-H-A-R-T-R-E-S.'

As Menéndez laboriously filled in the answer, Docherty took a good look round the spacious lobby. Over in the far corner an old man in a suit was watching a muted TV, but there were no other signs of human activity.

'Isabel Rodríguez?' he asked again.

Menéndez swung round reluctantly to check out the line of key-hooks. 'She is out,' he said.

Damn, Docherty said to himself. 'I would like to leave a message,' he said. 'It concerns tours in the mountains for tourists.'

The Argentinian managed to convey both indifference and acquiescence with the same shrug.

'Do you have any paper?' Docherty asked, thinking that it would have been more intelligent to have written the note out first.

As Menéndez rummaged around under his counter the street door swung open with a clatter, and Docherty swung round, slightly faster than he intended.

The woman's stride barely faltered. She was about the right age, and fitted the rough description Hemmings had given them: five foot eight inches tall, around nine and a half stone, shoulder-length black hair, dark-brown eyes, sallow skin, attractive. She was certainly the latter, Docherty thought. 'Isabel Rodríguez?' he asked for the third time, smiling as he did so.

Only her eyes betrayed any sense of alarm. 'Yes?'

'We talked on the telephone about the mountain tours,' he went on, moving his body between her and Menéndez, so that the latter would miss any confusion on her part. He need not have bothered.

'Oh, yes,' she said. 'Señor . . . I am sorry, I have forgotten your name.'

'Ramírez,' Docherty said, using the first name that came into his head. She was impressive, he thought.

'Well, would you like to go out for a drink? Or I have some in my room.' She did not bother to wait for his answer. 'Manuel, can I have my key.'

A minute later she was closing the door behind her and looking at him with a mixture of exasperation and anger. She did not need this, she thought, not today. Nor did she really want to know what he wanted from her.

'Can I pour us a drink?' Docherty asked, still speaking Spanish, and indicating the whisky on the bedside table. He felt he had earned it, after the last week or so.

'Just for yourself,' she said. 'What is your real name?' she asked, also in Spanish.

'Docherty. Jamie Docherty.'

Her lips creased in a faint smile, as if she was remembering something. She really was beautiful, he decided, but there seemed to be only sadness in her eyes.

'Miss Rodríguez,' he began, 'I have simply come to warn you. Our other patrol, outside Rio Grande – there has been no radio contact for almost twenty-four hours, and there is a good chance that they have been captured.'

She looked at him steadily.

'They have your name,' he said, 'as I think you know.'

'I was told.' She shrugged, and decided to pour herself a drink after all. 'Will they betray me?' she asked.

He started to say no, but stopped himself. If Wacko's feelings were reflected anywhere in Brookes's patrol, then maybe they would not be as careful as they should be. 'I don't know,' he said, looking straight at her. 'I doubt it, but I don't know.'

'Not even under torture,' she asked, almost aggressively.

'You probably know the answer to that better than I do,' he said simply. He put the empty glass down and got up. 'I just came to tell you what has happened. We are leaving tonight, for Chile. You can come with us if you want.'

Isabel studied his face, thinking that he might be a good man, without knowing why she thought so. 'No,' she said, 'I'll be all right.' The faint smile appeared again. 'Or maybe not,' she said, more to herself than to him. 'This is my home,' she added, realizing that some explanation was required.

216

'I understand,' he said. 'I'll be on my way.'

She started to move aside, but suddenly the thought of being left alone in that room was more than she could face. 'I can drive you out of town,' she said. 'It'll be safer.'

He hesitated. 'Are you sure?' he asked.

'Sure it will be safer? Yes.'

'Not for you.'

Maybe the SAS were English gentlemen after all, she thought. And maybe the Junta sent donations to Amnesty International. 'Let me worry about my safety,' she said brusquely. 'Do you have a map?'

He took it out, and showed her the spot where the road ran closest to the OP. 'I'll drop you there,' she said, as if they were popping into town together for a Saturday morning's shopping.

9

Once Docherty had disappeared into the darkness, Ben and Wacko had dozed off while Razor kept watch. Every few minutes he would diligently scan the distant airbase with the telescope, but the day's activity seemed over. Maybe they were simply licking their wounds, Razor thought. A lot more aircraft had flown out that day than had returned, and though it was possible that the missing planes had landed elsewhere, the messages from Hemmings suggested that most of them were headed for the ocean floor.

'There's no smoke without valour,' Razor murmured to himself, and smiled in the dark.

He thought about home and his mum and the house in Walthamstow. He wondered if she would like Corinna. Probably – his mum had a do-gooder streak in her about a mile wide, and she was getting pretty choosy about food these days. All those unsaturated poly-somethings. He sighed. It probably all made a lot of sense, but there was no doubt in his mind that beans on toast tasted better with white bread and proper butter.

He picked up the telescope again, just at the moment the noise of the helicopter became audible. The airbase still looked dead to the world, but the scrape of the chopper blades was growing louder.

And then he heard what sounded suspiciously like a cough somewhere out on the hillside.

It was too early for the boss to be back. Razor used his foot to wake Ben and Wacko. By the time they had joined him, their heads almost side by side to see through the observation slit, the helicopter was less than 200 yards away, trailing a spotlight beneath it, as if looking for the star performer on the huge stage of the Patagonian hillside.

It came to a hovering halt directly above them, flooding the roof of the hide with light.

But the voice, when it came, seemed to come from further down the slope. 'English soldiers,' it said, with a clarity of amplified sound which put Spurs' PA system to shame. 'You must leave your weapons and come out of your trench,' the voice went on. 'There are 100 soldiers all around you, so please do not try to be heroes.'

'Are there?' Razor muttered. 'Shall we try the back way out?' he asked the others.

'Yeah, let's be heroes,' Wacko said.

Ben nodded grimly.

'Ready?' Razor asked, as the amplifier began booming once more.

They were.

'One, two, three, go,' Razor barked, and all three men launched themselves through the turf roof and out onto the hillside, rolling free of the hide and springing to their feet in what seemed almost one continuous motion.

They were barely on their feet when one searchlight went on behind them, another burst into blinding light directly in their chosen path of escape, and someone opened fire with an SMG. Wacko went down like a sack of potatoes, two bullets in his chest and shoulder. The other two threw themselves down beside him to avoid a similar fate.

Two more searchlights burst into life on either side, and the helicopter seemed almost close enough above them to touch. When the Argies surround you, Razor thought, they do it with a vengeance.

Wacko was still conscious, but he seemed to be gritting his teeth with pain.

'Why spend the night out here when we have beds waiting for you?' the amplified voice boomed, just about audible above the helicopter.

'I'm going to stand up,' Razor told Ben. 'If the bastards shoot me, then try and take a few of them with you. If it comes to talking, don't let on we speak Spanish.' He took a deep breath and lifted himself slowly to his feet, hands held high, half-expecting any moment to feel the bullets cutting through him.

None came.

Ben stood up too, but still there was no gunfire. The helicopter was now moving away, its work apparently done.

'Our *amigo* is injured,' Razor shouted in English.

A couple of enemy troops rushed forward, SMGs at the ready, to cover them. The officer in charge, a paunchy colonel, followed at a more leisurely pace, growling orders at his subordinates, two of whom started tearing off the roof of the hide. He was accompanied by a cold-eyed man in plain clothes, and it was the latter who did the talking.

'You are so confident, you English,' Solanille told them in their own language. 'You think we are a Third World country, we cannot have thermal imaging, so you are quite safe in the dark.'

220

He walked over to look down on the exposed entrails of the hide. 'Impressive,' he said, and turned back to them. 'A cross has four arms, and there are four large bags here. But only three of you.'

'Our friend needs medical help,' Razor told him.

'Yes, he does,' Solanille said, looking down at Wacko without sympathy. He gestured to the colonel to do something, and turned back to Razor. 'He will receive help. Now where is the fourth man?'

'There is no fourth man,' Razor said. 'We have one bag each for our kit, and one for the radio.'

'And that is standard practice?' Solanille asked.

'It is standard practice,' Razor replied. SAS men were taught not to use simple yes or no replies, since these could be most easily used for the doctoring of tapes. Razor doubted whether this conversation on the hillside was being recorded, but he was not taking any chances. He did not want his mum listening to him apparently admitting to some atrocity or other on the BBC news. She was ambivalent enough about the SAS as it was.

'Ah. Then perhaps you can explain why the other patrol had four men?'

'Which other patrol?' Razor asked. He did not like the sound of all this one little bit, and he liked the look of this man even less. Still, he thought, at least they were lifting Wacko onto a stretcher rather than shooting him.

'The Rio Grande patrol,' Solanille said. 'One man is dead, two captured, one . . . we don't know. He is probably hiding in a hole like this one, wondering what to do next.'

'We have no knowledge of another patrol,' Razor said.

The Argentian smiled at him coldly. 'And I suppose your Queen Mother is a virgin,' he said contemptuously. He turned away. 'We shall continue this discussion in a nice warm room,' he said over his shoulder. 'Bring them.'

They drove slowly out of Rio Gallegos and onto the road signposted for Cabo Virgenes. Docherty found himself conscious of the movement of her thighs as she changed gears, and wondered whether she had had a boyfriend in England. If so, he guessed, then she must have left him without much explanation.

'Where are you from?' he asked

'Originally? Ushuaïa, it's in Tierra . . .'

'I know where it is.'

'Have you ever been there?'

'No.'

'It's the end of the world,' she said, almost proudly.

'Oh, I've been to several of them,' he said, with a lightness which seemed to emphasize its opposite.

She found herself believing him. This was not the sort of man she had expected from the SAS. 'Did you serve in Northern Ireland?' she asked, switching to English.

'Aye,' Docherty said. It seemed churlish, not to say childish, to deny the truth to a woman who was driving him around behind enemy lines.

'Don't you think Ireland should be one country?' she asked, and immediately wondered why she was asking such a man such a question in such a situation. It was completely crazy.

He seemed not to mind. 'I understand the desire,' he said. 'I'm a Glasgow Catholic – how could I not?

222

But I guess ... I guess I've come to believe that fighting to get things changed often ends up causing more harm than just learning to live with things the way they are.'

Isabel thought about it.

'And I think people who blow up pubs should be locked up,' he added, almost as an afterthought, 'no matter what they kid themselves they're doing it for.'

'Sometimes the way things are ...' she began. 'Sometimes it's so bad that there's no choice but to fight.'

'That I can believe,' he agreed. 'I guess wisdom is knowing which is which.'

'A soldier-philosopher,' she said, only half-ironic-ally.

He chose to take it straight. 'We are all many things,' he said. He could feel Liam McCall looking over his shoulder.

'We must be nearly there,' she said.

'About another half a mile,' he said. 'Over this ...'

He was silenced by the array of lights visible on the road ahead.

'They've seen us, so we have to go on,' she said calmly.

'OK,' he said, feeling for the Browning's grip in his pocket. The next few hundred yards seemed to take forever. Slowly the details behind the lights became clearer. There were several vehicles and a multitude of men in uniform.

A soldier stepped out to check them, but waved them on when he saw Isabel's worried face, and they drove slowly past the two armoured personnel carriers drawn up by the side of the road, and the two cars beyond them. Two men were being hustled aboard one of the former, and Docherty recognized Razor's unmistakable profile. In the light offered by one car's headlights Isabel saw Solanille standing talking to another officer.

'Your companions?' she asked, as the car crested the next shallow rise and began down another long slope.

'Aye,' Docherty said bitterly.

'I'm going to keep going for a mile or so,' she said. 'And then we'll have to sit for a while. I don't want to have to pass them again – it'll look too suspicious.'

'I can't believe they didn't stop us anyway,' Docherty said.

'In England they would have,' she said. 'Here they prefer to keep the ordinary citizen as far away as possible from such things. Once he saw I was a woman – and therefore nothing to do with anything military – he just wanted us out of there.'

A couple of minutes later she pulled the car over and switched off the lights. 'We can just keep going,' she said. 'I can get you to within a couple of miles of the border, and you can be across before first light.'

'No,' he said, almost absent-mindedly. Christ, what a cock-up, he thought. All their gear would have been taken, except for what he was carrying himself: one pair of PNGs, a telescopic night-sight, his knife, the Browning High Power, and the contents of his escape belt. 'Have you any idea where they'll be taken?' he asked Isabel.

'Maybe the airbase. Maybe the Intelligence HQ in town. You're not thinking of trying to rescue them?' she asked incredulously.

'I'm not leaving until I'm sure it's impossible,' he said.

She did not know what to say. Or do. Think, she told herself.

'Is there another way back into the town?' he asked.

'No. We'll have to wait And I'm not at all sure I want to drive you back into town. Or myself, for that matter.'

'I can understand that,' he said. 'And I can walk if necessary. But I'll need some directions.'

'Let me think for a minute,' she said, wishing she had some alcohol in the car. She had a definite feeling that time was running out for her in Rio Gallegos, but where was the feeling coming from? Several directions. There was the possibility that the captured SAS men would give her away, the fact that her face had been seen driving past by the soldier, Docherty's visit to her hotel. When Menéndez heard the news the next day that English spies had been captured would he start putting two and two together? Probably not, but still . . .

And anyway, what was the point of her staying? At the rate the English were shooting down planes the war could not last much longer. And her primary source of information was probably dead. Unless she had a death-wish – a not inconceivable hypothesis, she admitted to herself – it was time for her to get out.

Would she have a better chance with this man or without him? That was hard to say. With him, probably – at least until they were clear of Rio Gallegos. Then alone

In the seat next to her Docherty was also wondering what he should do. As he saw it, he had three options:

to head for the border with this woman, to head back into town with her, or to send her on towards the border while he headed back into town on his own. The last option, while the least appealing from most points of view, unfortunately seemed the one demanded by his sense of duty.

'Look,' he said. 'If they catch me there's a good chance I'll be treated as a prisoner of war, or at the worst as some sort of hostage. If they catch you they'll probably hang you, or whatever they do to traitors in this country. So you should keep going, and try and get across the border. I know where the airbase is, so just tell me where to find this Intelligence HQ.'

This, she thought, was one of those rare moments when you got to choose. It was like a fork in the road of her life. If she went one way she would have one type of life, if she went the other it would all turn out completely differently. Crossing the border might mean safety, but it would also mean the end of any chance for her to resurrect her soul.

It was melodramatic as hell, she thought, but true all the same.

She turned to face Docherty. 'I'm not going to try and explain,' she said, 'because there isn't time and I don't think you'd understand in any case. But this is my war too, and I've been fighting it, either here or in my head in England, for ten years. Most of my friends are dead, and the thought of joining them lost its sting a long time ago. You see, I could cross ten borders and not leave this war behind, so let's just get on with it.'

In the gloom her face was decidedly madonna-like, he thought, all holiness and suffering and self-denial. He felt infinitely sorry for her, and, at

226

the same time, drawn to her to more strongly than he wanted to be.

'I hear you,' he said. 'So which do we go for first – the airbase or town?'

'Town,' she said decisively. 'If we go cruising round the airbase at this time of night there's a ninety per cent chance we'll be stopped by someone or other. And I think it's more likely they'll be taken into town,' she added. With Solanille, she told herself. With Solanille.

She started the Renault, did a U-turn, and set off slowly back the way they had come, all lights off. At the top of the rise they could see that the APCs and cars had all gone, leaving just the open lorry. But there was no sign of human life.

'They must be waiting for you,' she said. 'You'd better get in the back seat, as far down as you can.'

Docherty packed as much of himself into the narrow gap as he could and waited, Browning at the ready, as they descended the slope.

'Nobody there,' she said a few moments later.

He climbed back into the front seat and watched the few remaining lights of Rio Gallegos draw steadily closer.

Razor and Ben had endured a long, jolting ride in the back of an armoured personnel carrier, surrounded by Argentinian soldiers who obviously felt they had accomplished the moral equivalent of kidnapping Mrs Thatcher. Still, they were obviously not a bad bunch of lads, Razor thought, listening to them chatting excitedly to each other. He would have liked to have thanked them for giving Ardiles and Villa to Spurs, but the need to conceal his knowledge

227

of Spanish rendered a harmless conversation about football impossible.

He wondered how and where Wacko was. The head honcho in plain clothes had told them their comrade was being taken to the local hospital, but Razor and Ben had no way of knowing if he was speaking the truth. The only certainty was that Wacko was not with them.

After what seemed like half an hour, but was probably less, the APC slowed to a halt, and then reversed. The rear door opened onto a view of a wall with a door in it. The two SAS men, who had been handcuffed before getting aboard, were hustled out by two armed soldiers, and had time to glimpse a lighted street before the door closed behind them and their escort.

They were in a house, or at least an official building, not a barracks or military detention centre. A carpeted corridor led through to what looked like the lobby, where a uniformed man sat in front of several TV screens. They were guided past a room full of desks and office equipment and up a wide staircase, also richly carpeted. A chandelier hung in the stairwell.

Razor turned to Ben, whose face, like his own, was still covered with camouflage cream. 'Do you think they'll be able to lend us a couple of tuxedos?' he asked.

'*Silencio*,' said one of the guards with no great conviction.

They were prodded into an extremely spacious room on the first floor. A large polished table occupied the centre of the floor, but there were no accompanying chairs and it seemed to serve no purpose other than to support a large vase of flowers. Three ornate chairs sat beneath the three large windows, which were concealed by floor-length maroon velvet curtains with golden tassels. Razor remembered Spike Milligan's line: 'The curtains were drawn but the room was real.'

Solanille was sitting at a large desk in one corner of the room, talking on the telephone. A few feet away the flames of a coal fire were dancing happily in a Victorian-style grate. Above the mantlepiece was the portrait of a general with bright-blue eyes and a mouth like a man-trap.

'And the one who got away?' Solanille was asking in Spanish. Razor tried not to give any clue that he understood what was being said.

'Have you questioned the prisoner?' Solanille asked. His face betrayed frustration at the answer he was getting. 'Yes, yes, I understand,' he said, 'we have a similar problem here . . . yes, Luis, I will talk to you in a couple of hours.' He put the phone down and looked at the two handcuffed SAS men.

Razor noticed for the first time that there were three Browning High Powers sitting on the desk, presumably his, Ben's and Wacko's. 'May I say something?' he asked.

Solanille grunted his acquiescence.

'What is your name and rank?' Razor asked.

Solanille frowned. 'Neither my name nor my position are of any concern to you,' he said.

'It is a courtesy usually accorded prisoners of war,' Razor said, sure he had heard the line before, probably in some crappy war film.

The Argentinian laughed. 'No uniform, no declaration of war – you will be treated as the terrorists you are,' he said. 'Your friends in Tierra del Fuego killed nine men,' he went on, 'and murder carries the death penalty in Argentina.'

Razor and Ben said nothing.

'We have checked out your equipment and clothes,' Solanille said, 'and it is obvious that there are four of you. Where is the fourth man?'

'There are only three of us,' Razor said.

Solanille shrugged. 'We shall see.'

'Ve have vays of making you talk, Englischer schwein,' Razor muttered under his breath. And they probably did. He felt more than a little uneasy. In fact, he admitted to himself, he felt bloody scared.

It was almost midnight now, but the streets of Rio Gallegos were far from deserted. 'Friday night,' Isabel explained, as a group of drunken oil workers lurched across the road in front of them.

'Just like Peterhead,' Docherty muttered.

She drove slowly down Avenida Julio Roca and came to a halt outside the hotel. 'I need to get something before we do anything else,' she said.

He opened his mouth to ask her whether whatever it was was really necessary, then closed it again.

She saw his hesitation. 'If by some miracle we can free your friends,' she explained, 'we can't just head for the border by the quickest route. We wouldn't get ten miles. So we're going to need money, and I don't suppose you're carrying many spare pesos.'

'No,' Docherty admitted. 'But I hear you're pretty good at robbing banks.'

She almost smiled, and reached for the door. 'If I'm more than ten minutes,' she said, 'take the car.'

Docherty sat watching the wide and mostly empty avenue. Pedestrians in pairs and groups wandered by, and an occasional car or taxi. The police were conspicuous by their absence. No one paid him any mind.

Isabel reappeared, carrying one small bag. 'I decided a change of clothing would be nice,' she said.

'I know what you mean,' Docherty said wryly.

She started the car. 'How far away should we park?' she asked.

'You know the place. How does around the nearest corner sound?'

'As good as anywhere.' She slipped the car into gear and pulled out in the wake of a cruising taxi. 'By the way,' she added, 'it's opposite the city police station.'

'Jesus,' Docherty murmured.

This time she did smile, and swung the Renault left down Calle Corrientes, across Calle Zapiola and right down Calle Libertad. In the middle of the second block she pulled up, and pointed at the house on her right. 'It's behind that, in the next street,' she said. The excitement of it all was beginning to get to her, as it had always done all those years ago.

They got out of the car, conscious of the emptiness of the street. 'I think it might be an idea if we tried to look like we're fond of each other,' Docherty said, putting his arm round her shoulder.

She hesitated for only a second before slipping an arm around his waist. 'Christ, when did you last have a wash?' she asked a few paces later.

'About a week ago.'

'As recently as that?'

They turned into Calle Ameghino and walked the block to Calle Zapiola. The police station on the far side of the road seemed dead to the world. 'This way,'

she whispered, leading him to the right. 'Stop for a
kiss in front of the second building.' Docherty did
what he was told, kissing her lightly on the mouth
before burying her head in his shoulder, and staring
across the top of her head at the building as he ran
his fingers through her hair.

'What can you see?' she whispered impatient-
ly.

'A lot of curtains drawn across lighted windows,'
he said. 'A uniform in the lobby watching screens.
But there's no way of knowing if they're in there.
Let's move.'

They resumed their progress, walking past a side
entrance for vehicles. Docherty had a momentary
glimpse of an illuminated yard, complete with surveillance camera above a lit doorway.

They turned right again. 'Any ideas?' he asked.

Isabel was remembering a very similar building in
Córdoba, and a very similar problem, in the summer
of 1974. 'There's only one way in,' she said. 'Through
the front door.'

'We just go and knock?'

'Not quite. I go and look lost. Get the guard out here
and . . . Or we could abseil in through the windows,'
she added sarcastically.

'I prefer the first idea,' Docherty said. They discussed the details for a few moments, as they embraced
on the pavement beside the car. 'Are you sure you can
do this?' Docherty asked one more time.

Her face was expressionless. 'Like you said, it's the
death penalty if I'm caught.'

'Then let's do it.'

Five minutes later she was standing in front of the
glass doors of the Intelligence building, using mime to

persuade the guard within that she needed help with some terrible problem.

Docherty watched from behind the porch, thinking how good she was, and wondering if her nerve would hold. He would have done it himself, but there was no way he could have got as close.

He could not see the guard, who was looking at her, then at the screens, and then at her again. She was gorgeous, the guard thought. Her coat was open and the swell of her breasts beneath the sweater almost brought a lump to his throat. And she looked so lost.

He came across to the door, and opened it a few inches.

She pulled Docherty's silenced Browning out of her coat pocket and shot him through the heart.

He went down with more noise than she had expected, but no other guards appeared to investigate. The two of them slipped inside, and she closed the doors behind her while Docherty dragged the guard's body back to the seat in front of the TV console, and propped it up as well as he could manage. The screens showed several views of the outside world, and two of the building's inner workings. Both these latter offered a fisheye-lens view of landings, which could only be those on the two floors above them. The top landing was empty, but the one immediately above them contained two seated guards, neither wearing uniform but both armed with SMGs.

From the screen it looked as though this landing was four-sided, like a balcony around a courtyard, and that the two guards were sitting in opposite corners, one facing the top of the stairs leading up from the lobby, the other out of sight to the rear.

Killing the first man would be easy enough, but getting to the second before he raised the alarm was going to be tricky.

Docherty thought for a moment, then outlined a plan.

'OK,' Isabel nodded.

He put his hand out for the Browning, and she reluctantly handed it back. Then it occurred to her to remove the dead guard's handgun from his leather police holster.

'Only as a last resort,' he told her.

She concealed it in her coat pocket and gave him a withering 'what kind of a fool do you take me for?' look. He shrugged an apology. They moved down a short corridor, and started up the long staircase, Isabel in the lead, hands grasped behind her back. Docherty brought up the rear, holding the gun on her.

They were about sixteen steps from the top when the first guard's head appeared in view. He stared first at her, and then at Docherty, with the same questioning look.

'She is an accomplice of the English spies,' Docherty told him abruptly, as if he was generously providing more explanation than the guard was due.

They were only ten steps from the top now, and the second guard would be coming into Docherty's possible line of fire.

'I have not . . .' the first guard started to say, and Docherty put a double tap through his forehead, whirling almost in the same instant in search of the other target.

The second guard was still standing open-mouthed when two bullets in the upper trunk punched him back into the chair he had just vacated.

A loud thump announced the first guard's meeting

with the floor. There were sounds in the room behind him, first of a voice, then of footsteps. Docherty and Isabel stepped swiftly forward, reaching either side of the door just as it opened.

A man stepped out, gun in hand. He had time for one surprised *qué*? before Docherty shot him through the head.

The SAS man stepped through the door, his Browning seeking out more targets. A man behind a desk sat perfectly still, another man's gun hit the floor as his hands reached up, and Docherty's two SAS partners grinned from ear to ear.

'What you been doing, boss – sightseeing?' Razor complained. He suddenly noticed Isabel standing behind Docherty. 'Don't answer that. We understand completely.'

'Where's Wacko?' Docherty asked. He noticed the two men were handcuffed. 'And where are the keys for those?'

'The keys are in his pocket,' Ben said, indicating the guard with his hands up. 'But we don't know where Wacko is. He took two bullets when we were captured. They say they took him off to hospital.'

'He was in bad shape, boss,' Razor said. 'There's no way he could travel.'

'He is being treated at the airbase you have been spying on,' Solanille told them, ingratiatingly. He became conscious that the woman was staring at him.

'Do you remember me, Señor Solanille?' she asked, walking slowly towards him.

'No,' he said. 'I do not have the habit of associating with traitors.'

She picked up one of the three silenced Brownings lying on the desk.

'What's going on, boss?' Razor asked Docherty.

The PC shook his head. 'It's her business,' he said. And unless she jeopardized their safety he had no intention of interfering.

'You sent me to the Naval Mechanical School,' Isabel was telling Solanille in a voice that sent a shiver down Docherty's spine.

The Argentinian's face expressed sudden recognition.

Isabel rammed the Browning's barrel into his genitals.

He cried out once in shock, and then looked up her with pleading eyes as her finger tightened on the trigger. 'No,' he whimpered. 'I never . . .'

'You never dirtied your own hands,' she said, held his eyes for what must been the longest seconds of his life, and then suddenly lifted the gun and whipped it fast and hard across his face, drawing a cascade of blood from his nose. She turned abruptly on her heel and told Docherty: 'Let's get out of here.'

'Take it easy,' he said gently, and watched her take a deep breath. 'We'll be gone as soon as we can.' He turned to Razor and Ben. 'Should we kill these two?'

The two troopers said nothing.

'If it was for the sake of the mission, I'd say yes,' Docherty said. 'But since we'd only be killing them to increase our chances of getting away . . .' He looked at the other two. 'I'd rather we just took our chances.'

'Sounds good to me,' Ben said.

Razor agreed.

'Tie them up, then. The curtain cords will do.' Docherty walked over to where Isabel was standing by the door. 'Any sign of life?'

'None,' she said.

'Which direction should we take?' he asked.

'If we get out of here without being seen, then south. We can be at the border in two hours.'

'Good. This Naval Mechanical School – what was it?' Docherty asked.

'It was a torture chamber,' she said.

'I thought it might . . .' he started to say, but Razor's warning shout had him stepping to the right and bringing up the Browning as his eyes sought the threat. He saw the automatic in Solanille's hand at the moment of detonation, and as the echoes of the crack merged into a cry of pain from Isabel he put a bullet through the Argentinian's left eye.

The surviving guard threw himself on the floor.

'No need to tie him up now,' Razor said, looking down at Solanille.

Docherty was examining Isabel's wound, and cursing himself for not being more careful. Her presence was not helping his concentration, he realized, and it was she who had paid the price. Why the fuck had he not thought to use the handcuffs?

'Just handcuff and gag the guard,' Docherty told Ben. Talk about locking the stable door after the horse has bolted.

'How is she, boss?' Razor asked, kneeling down beside them. He was the patrol's specialist medic, but Docherty had had almost as much medical training.

'I'll live,' she said, trying to prop herself up on one elbow. 'The moral of this story is don't threaten to shoot off a soldier's dick,' she said weakly.

'We are kind of attached to them,' Razor murmured. 'But you stay put for a moment,' he added, gently pushing her back down. He used his knife to cut away the blood-soaked section of her dress between breast and shoulder. The bullet had gone clean through, and he doubted whether there was any severe damage, but she was losing a lot of blood.

'Trouble, boss,' Ben said from the window. Docherty went across to join him. Two uniformed men were standing on the steps of the police station across the street, staring in the direction of the building they were in.

'They must have heard the shot,' Ben said. As he said it another man came out and the three of them started walking across the street.

'Shit,' Docherty said emphatically. 'Take the top of the stairs, Ben,' he said, and walked swiftly across to where the surviving guard was still lying face down, handcuffed, on the carpet. 'Is there a back way out of here?' Docherty asked him in Spanish.

The man looked up at him with an expression half-terrified, half-defiant.

'A bargain,' Docherty said, 'your life for a back way out.' He tried to look as if he did not much care what the answer was.

The man swallowed once. '*Sí*,' he said, 'I will show you.' Docherty pulled the man to his feet, and saw that Razor had got Isabel to hers. She looked deadly pale, and her face seemed pinched with the effort required to stay conscious.

'You'd better carry her,' Docherty told Razor. 'Let's go,' he said to the guard.

They emerged onto the landing just as Ben opened up with his silenced Browning. In the stairwell there was the sound of someone either jumping or falling back down the stairs, and a few choice Spanish epithets. Presumably the discovery of the dead guard at the console had already resulted in a general alarm.

Fools rush in, but you can't make them drink, Razor thought to himself, as the guard led them down a short corridor towards the rear of the building, and down a wrought-iron spiral staircase to a back door.

Ben opened it gingerly, and poked an eye round the corner. He could see and hear nothing.

They all emerged into a back yard. Across a six-foot wall two large houses were silhouetted against the night sky. It was topped by lines of razor wire, and Docherty was wondering how the fuck they were going to get Isabel across, when Ben announced the discovery of a gate.

'The escape gate,' the guard explained helpfully.

Ben had already shot away the padlock. The open gate revealed a narrow passage running between the two houses.

'Go!' Docherty told Ben and Razor. He turned to the guard, whose face seemed about to break up in fear. '*Muchas gracias, señor,*' Docherty told him, and closed the door in his face.

He ran down the passage in pursuit of the others, catching them at the opening onto the street. The Renault was still standing where they had left it, only 20 yards away.

'That's what I call planning, boss,' Razor said admiringly. He helped Isabel into the back seat and climbed in beside her. Docherty told Ben to drive. 'Just get us a few streets away,' he said.

Ben pulled away from the kerb, and Docherty turned to face Isabel. 'Which way?' he asked her.

She looked at him blankly for a moment, then her eyes came back into focus. 'Calafate,' she said.

'Where . . .'

'There's a map in the glove compartment,' she said.

'Where the hell's Calafate?' Ben asked.

'It's about 150 miles to the north-west,' Docherty said, examining the map. 'Not that far from the mountains and the Chilean border. And she's right – the whole Argentinian military will be looking for us in about half an hour's time. This border's a lot further away, but there'll be some cover. The road to the southern border is just flat and empty, like a target range. We'd never have made it.'

The other two absorbed this information. 'Join the SAS and see the world,' Ben murmured. 'So which way?' he asked, taking another turn to the right. He liked the idea of seeing some mountains again.

Behind him Isabel was remembering Calafate, which she had visited two weeks before as part of her cover job. It was a beautiful place, she thought, as she drifted into unconsciousness.

'Pull over for a minute,' Docherty told Ben. 'I want to know what we're doing before we hit the open road.' He squirmed round in his seat. 'How is she?' he asked Razor.

'Out like a light, but I think she'll be OK. There's not much I can do without any kit. I'd like to wash the wound though, first chance we get.'

Docherty looked at her. The face was still pale, but he had no reason to doubt Razor's diagnosis. Solanille's bullet had not killed her, but if his friends caught up with them then they probably would. And it did not look like she would be up to climbing any mountains for a while. Which meant . . .

'We need another car,' he said abruptly.

'What's wrong with this one?' Ben asked, surprised.

'Nothing. I meant an additional car. As in two.' He sorted out his thoughts. 'Look,' he told the two men, 'according to this map, four or five hours' drive should get us within a few hours hard hiking of the Chilean border. But there's no way she's going to be able to do any hiking at all, and we can't leave her behind. If it wasn't for her, you two would still be back there,' he added.

'OK, boss, but . . .'

'Just listen for once in your insubordinate life. If she and I can get to Calafate then there's a good chance we can pass ourselves off as a married couple or something. But if all four of us drive in then it'll look like an invasion. You two have camouflage trousers on, for Christ's sake . . .'

'You don't look that elegant yourself, boss . . .'

'Meanwhile you two can take this road,' Docherty insisted, showing it to them on the map, 'dump the car somewhere round here' – he pointed out a particular spot – 'and get the hell out of this fucking country.'

Ben and Razor said nothing.

'Well?' Docherty asked.

'Boss,' Razor began tentatively, 'you're not getting carried away by, well . . .' He nodded towards Isabel.

Docherty grinned at him. 'Who the fuck knows? The point is, can either of you clowns think of a better plan for giving all four of us a chance?'

They could not.

'Right, we've been here long enough. Let's find another car.'

They found an anonymous-looking black VW Beetle closer to the outskirts, parked on a convenient slope, its doors unlocked. Razor freewheeled it down the slope, and then hot-wired the engine. The sound seemed to carry alarmingly.

'The Renault's tank is almost full,' Ben said. 'What about yours?' he asked Razor.

'Better than half.'

'Follow us,' Docherty told him. 'I want to make some improvements, but let's get out of town first.'

He directed Ben down a wide, dusty street, looking for the large lagoon shown on the map. It appeared, black and still, reflecting a few dim yellow lights on its far shore. They came to a crossroads and followed the signs for Ruta 3 and the north, passing two cars and a full coach going in the opposite direction. The estuary appeared to their right, though it was hard to work out how wide it was. Clouds had driven in from the west and the stars had all been extinguished.

'If you see somewhere to turn off, take it,' Docherty told Ben.

They eventually found a turning, and less than a minute later found themselves in a car park for a picnic area by the side of the estuary. The three men got out.

'Have we really got time for a picnic, boss?' Razor asked in a concerned voice.

Docherty was looking back towards the city, where a light seemed to be bobbing in the dull black sky. It was a helicopter. 'Disconnect all the lighting in the Beetle,' he told Razor. 'I'll drive the Renault,' he explained to the two of them as Razor started

242

work, 'with lights full on. You two should be able
to follow the road by my lights. If we're spotted from
the air, then, provided the night stays as dark as this,
they should only see the front car. If they land on the
road up ahead then you two hang back. If they believe
it's me and the missus on our way to the mountains
for a holiday, well and good. If they don't, then you
two will have surprise on your side when it comes to
rescuing us. Got it?'

'A masterplan, boss,' Razor murmured. 'The chopper's headed our way,' he added, almost as an
afterthought. All three men watched it head up the
highway they had driven out on, and pass low above
the turning they had taken 200 yards away.

'We've got time for you to wash her wound,'
Docherty told Razor.

'OK.' The Londoner found a way down to the river
and soaked a piece of cloth in the near-freezing water.
Back in the Renault, its application brought Isabel
back to life, if only for a couple of minutes.

'Qué pasa . . .?'

'I'm just cleaning up the wound,' Razor said in
Spanish.

She winced as he dragged dry blood away with
the cloth. Still, at least that meant the bleeding had
stopped. 'Where are we?' she asked.

'Just outside Rio Gallegos.'

'And going to Calafate?'

'So I'm told. You'd be better sleeping,' he told her.
'Let us worry about the travel arrangements.'

She managed a hint of a smile. To rely on the
English SAS for escape from her own country – how
many ironies could one situation contain? She closed
her eyes.

Razor noticed the car clock, which said it was almost two. Add three hours for the time difference, he thought. The Cup Final was only ten hours away. He hoped Hoddle was having a better night's sleep than they were.

Outside the car Ben and Docherty were staring into space.

'All finished,' Razor said. 'We can go now,' he explained patiently.

'I was hoping to see that helicopter again before we moved,' Docherty said. 'But . . .'

Its light appeared in the western sky, and soon the accompanying drone of its engine seeped out of the silence. A minute later it was sweeping past them, still hugging the highway, this time heading back towards the town.

'Brilliant,' Docherty said to no one in particular. 'Let's go.' He climbed into the front seat of the Renault, took one look at the sleeping Isabel in the back seat, and started the engine. A minute later they were on Ruta 3 again, the Renault showing all its lights, the VW travelling just behind the limits of the other car's aura. It worked well: even knowing there was something to look for, Docherty could often see no sign of the VW in his rear mirror.

In the six miles to the Calafate turn-off they passed only two vehicles, both trucks, headed in the opposite direction, and once on the narrower Calafate road they seemed to be almost alone in the universe. To either side of the road the darkness stretched away, not yielding a single light for miles on end. They could have been traversing a desert, travelling through a tall forest or crossing an endless bridge. It felt more like a tunnel than anything else. For Ben, struggling without lights to keep the VW inside the tracks of the Renault, it sometimes seemed more like a video game than a real drive.

In the car ahead, Docherty was trying to calculate times and distances. It was one-fifteen when they left the Intelligence building, which meant that they could have been at the southern border around an hour later. How long would it take the Argentinians to realize that they were not on that road? Another couple of hours, perhaps. And then what would they do? Widen the search, and keep widening it? But they did not have an unlimited supply of helicopters or pilots. And they were supposed to be fighting a war.

The telephone, he thought. The poles ran alongside the road. Cutting the wire might be a giveaway, but it might be worth it. No, he finally decided. He and the woman would be stuck this side of the border for a couple of days at least, and he could not afford to leave any more trail for the enemy to follow than they already had.

It took him a while, but eventually Hemmings managed to get through to Bryan Weighell's home in the suburbs of Hereford. It was midnight, but Weighell was still awake. The events of the day had served as continuing shots of adrenalin, and even two large malt whiskies had failed to slow him down.

'What's the news?' he asked Hemmings, marvelling yet again at the clarity of the connection.

'Mostly good.' Hemmings briefly outlined what he knew of the situation ashore on the first night, and the current condition of the SAS units on the islands.

'What about North and South?' Weighell wanted to know.

'That's the bad news, and that's what I'm calling you for . . .'

'What's happened now?' Weighell asked, a sinking feeling in his stomach.

'We've lost radio contact with both groups. You know about Brookes's patrol. Well, they may have taken out some Super Etendards – we've no way of knowing. There's been no sign of them today – the Super Es, I mean – which looks good. If Brookes and the other lads have managed to nobble them then they deserve knighthoods. But there's no news of them. They could be dead, captured, or just lying low somewhere without a radio.'

'And North?'

'No idea. They radioed in that Docherty was going into Rio Gallegos to warn the MI6 woman, and that once he returned they'd be heading for the border. They may be on their way, but we tried to raise them again an hour ago and couldn't. So . . .' He let the implications speak for themselves.

'You think they may have been captured,' Weighell said.

'I think there's a good chance some of those eight men have been taken,' Hemmings admitted.

Weighell rubbed his eyes. 'OK,' he said. 'I'll get onto it. Thanks for calling, Bill.'

He hung up, took the whisky over to his desk and sat down with a pen and paper. He needed a list of people to call, a list of people to pressure. Somehow, through any and every channel available to him – and even a few that were not – he had to get word through to those Argentinian authorities who were holding his men. The message would be twofold: one, that he expected his men to be accorded all the privileges and rights due to prisoners of war; and two, that there would be no escape from retribution for anyone who treated them otherwise.

Ten miles short of Esperanza, Docherty flashed his brake lights twice to indicate he was stopping, pulled over to the side of the road, and got out of the car. A landscape of undulating hills was dimly visible: either dawn was coming a lot earlier than he had expected or the cloud cover was imperceptibly thinning. The latter, he decided, studying the sky.

The VW pulled up behind the Renault, and the other two got out. 'What's up, Doc?' Razor asked.

'Nothing. I've just been doing some calculations in my head, and I reckon that at some point in the next hour there's a good chance they'll be checking this road again from the air.'

'Can we afford to hang around, boss?' Ben asked. 'It'll start to get light in a couple of hours.'

'I don't know – it's a toss-up. But a fifteen-minute break wouldn't do me any harm, and I don't suppose driving that thing without any lights is exactly relaxing.'

'Not for the poor passenger, it isn't,' Razor complained. 'I just sit there expecting Jim Clark here to drive us off a cliff any moment.'

'You've spent most of the time sleeping,' Ben said trenchantly.

'Thinking. Not sleeping.'

'He snores when he thinks,' Ben told Docherty.

Docherty grinned.

'How's the invalid?' Razor asked.

'She's asleep. And she looks OK. I . . .' The sound of a helicopter insinuated itself into his consciousness.

'Boss, you're a genius,' Razor sighed.

Docherty said nothing, but felt absurdly pleased that his calculations had proved so accurate.

The helicopter swept towards them, flew straight over their heads and on up the road towards Esperanza. If Docherty had not pulled up, the Renault's lights would undoubtedly have been spotted before he heard the approaching helicopter above the car engine.

'Ten minutes to Esperanza and back,' he murmured.

'Unless they land,' Ben suggested.

'Let's pray they don't.'

The minutes passed slowly, and it was more than fifteen before the whirr of the blades re-emerged, and the single pinpoint of light brightened as the helicopter approached. The black shape loomed out of the black sky, clattered above them and was gone again.

Docherty gave it a couple of minutes, and then pulled the Renault back onto the road. In fifteen minutes they were entering the small town of Esperanza, where, until the appearance of the helicopter, he had been most afraid of their finding a welcoming committee. But it seemed as if the military authorities in Rio Gallegos were keeping matters exclusively in their own hands, presumably as a way of handling the whole business with the minimum damage to their own credibility. Whatever the reason, Esperanza was fast asleep, and blissfully oblivious of the passage of fugitive SAS.

Ten miles or so beyond the town the roads to Calafate and the border at El Turbio diverged. The three men got out of the cars once more, but there was nothing really to say, except good luck and goodbye for the moment. Docherty gave them a portion of

248

Isabel's money, just in case. Then the two troopers solemnly shook hands with their PC.

'We'll be staying at the Santiago Hilton,' was Razor's parting shot through the window, as the VW rolled away into the darkness. Docherty stood by the Renault for a few seconds, savouring the moment. He had good mates, there was a beautiful woman in the back of his car, and he was standing in the dark in the middle of nowhere, hunted by the forces of the enemy.

It sure as hell beat feeling sorry for himself in the Slug & Sporran.

10

It started to get light as the VW clambered up the last few miles of the long valley. Clouds still filled the view behind them, diffusing the dawn sunlight, but to the west the sky was clearing again. As they breasted the last in a series of slopes, a vista of snow-capped mountains appeared in the far distance.

'The Andes,' Ben murmured.

'And there I was hoping it was the Chilterns,' Razor replied. He was driving now, and enjoying it a lot more since he had been able to see where he was going. The hour he had driven without lights of any kind had been a nightmare. It would probably have been quicker to have just sat in a lay-by, if they could have found one in the dark.

Ben was still taking in the view. 'You've got no soul,' he complained. This was the reason he was not prepared to give up the SAS, he thought.

'A mountain range is a mountain range. It's just a lot of rock in one place, that's all.'

Ben looked at him pityingly.

'OK, it is sort of . . . majestic,' Razor agreed. Corinna would love somewhere like this, he thought.

'It's also Chile,' Ben said. 'Over there, it is.' He gestured in the general direction of the west.

'Would you like to be a bit more precise,' Razor

suggested. 'Like, how far from the border are we, and how far on the other side can we expect to find a suitable hostelry?'

'I think pubs are pretty thin on the ground in southern Chile,' Ben observed. 'In a couple of miles this road takes a bloody great turn to the left, and after another couple we're about five miles from the border. It looks like a downhill walk. Unfortunately, there seems to be something like a 40-mile walk on the other side.'

'Downhill?'

'Mostly. On the other hand,' he continued, 'if we keep going till we're a few miles outside El Turbio, then the border's still only about five miles away, and the main road to Puerto Natales is only a couple of miles on the other side.'

'But is it all downhill?'

'For you, it's all downhill.'

'That's the one then.'

'Wake me up when we get there,' Ben said.

Razor ignored him. 'I wonder how the boss is getting on,' he said.

'You mean, has he had her yet?'

'No, I don't. Well, yes I do. But not as crudely as that. It was all a bit weird, don't you think?'

Ben considered. 'I don't know. What else could he have done? She's one of ours and he couldn't . . . ah, Docherty's always been . . . you know, his wife getting killed and all that . . . he . . .'

'Thank you, Dr Freud. I think I'll just go back to wondering if he's had her yet.'

The first hint of light was still colouring the sky when Docherty pulled up the Renault on the outskirts of

Calafate. It was obviously not a big town, but the plethora of helpful signs for the tourists suggested it saw a lot of custom in season. Unfortunately the season had ended a month ago, which might mean all the hotels were closed for the winter.

At least there were no signs of a welcoming committee, he thought, watching the view gradually unfold with the growing light. Calafate seemed fast asleep beside its beautiful lake. It was almost seven – not the best time to be searching for a hotel room, but late enough not to be waking everyone up. And he did not want to be sitting here by the side of the road much longer.

In the back seat Isabel was, as far as he could judge, breathing more or less normally. It was time to wake her up. He took her hand and gently squeezed it. Her eyes opened, and her other hand went lazily up to brush her hair away from them. Then she saw him, and awareness came flooding back. Her shoulder began to ache. 'Where are we?' she asked.

'Calafate. Just outside. I want to get us off the street and out of sight, and I need to know if you can walk OK.'

'I don't see why not,' she said. 'I wasn't shot in the legs.'

He helped her out of the car, and she took a few unsteady steps. 'I do feel weak,' she admitted.

'Eat this,' he said, giving her a small piece of chocolate from his emergency rations. 'It may make you buzz a bit.'

It did, but she felt stronger. 'Where are the others?' she asked.

'On the road to Puerto Natales. They're going to get as close as they can, then walk across into Chile.'

'And you stayed behind for me.' It was not so much a question as an expression of surprise.

'We try not to leave men behind,' he said, 'let alone women.'

She gave him a strange look, and tried walking a few more paces. As long as she put no demands on her upper body there was no extra pain. 'I'll be all right,' she said, walking round and manœuvring herself slowly into the vacant front seat.

Docherty got in behind the wheel. 'Have you been here before?' he asked.

'Two weeks ago.'

'That's good. Where did you stay?'

'The Hospedaje del Glaciar. On the lake. I'll show you.'

He started the car, and she guided him through the empty streets of the town, and down the slight slope to the lake, where several hotels seemed to be fighting for the best view. One, slightly removed from the rest, was built on a small peninsula which jutted out into the lake. It was painted white, had two storeys, and boasted a wide verandah overlooking the still waters.

They left the Renault in the small car park behind the hotel, and rang the old-fashioned bell hanging by the front door. It all felt more than a little unreal to Docherty: less than twelve hours had passed since he had left the OP overlooking the Rio Gallegos airbase.

A plump woman with a huge mane of black hair opened the door, and her scowl-in-waiting changed instantly to a smile when she saw Isabel.

The two women hugged, and Docherty saw Isabel wince with pain, but she betrayed nothing. 'Do you have a room for us for the weekend?' she asked. 'My fiancé and I,' she added, introducing Docherty by the first name that came into her head – Franco. 'He has come to stay with me in Rio Gallegos for a couple of weeks.'

She took a deep breath, and Docherty was afraid she was in danger of collapsing. 'We have been driving most of the night,' he explained, 'and Isabel is very tired. Could she lie down, do you think?'

'Yes, I'm exhausted,' Isabel confirmed.

The woman, whose name was Rosa, showed them up to one of the rooms which led out onto the verandah overlooking the lake. It was sparsely furnished but scrupulously clean.

'Breakfast is at eight,' she said, and left them.

Isabel sat down unsteadily on the side of the bed with a heartfelt sigh of relief, and tried to bring her legs up so she could lie down. It was harder than she expected. 'Can you help me?' she asked Docherty.

'First, I want to look at your wound,' he said.

'It feels OK,' she said.

'No arguments.'

She relented and sat patient-like on the side of the bed.

'I'll need to take off the blouse,' he said.

'This is one of those highly ambivalent scenes, isn't it?' she said, as he started to peel off her blouse. 'You take off my clothes and I wonder if your motives are purely medical.'

Docherty smiled. 'There's nothing ambivalent about it at all,' he said. 'My motives for taking off your clothes on this occasion are purely medical. And if I start taking them off on some other occasion there won't be any ambivalence there either,' he added.

'I think you're an extraordinary woman. And very sexy too.'

He examined the entry and exit wounds carefully, trying to be true to his words and not to get distracted by the swell of her breasts beneath the brassière.

'You're not what I expected, either,' she said. He was not exactly good looking, but there was something about the man that she responded to. Maybe she had finally cracked, she thought sourly.

'There doesn't seem to be any infection,' he said, 'but some hot water wouldn't be a bad idea. If there is any,' he added, looking round.

'There is,' she said. It was all in her never-to-be-published guide.

He soaked a convenient flannel and did as he had said, then helped her into a horizontal position and covered her with all the blankets he could find.

It was gone eight, and he felt ravenous. First, though, he badly needed a shower.

Ten minutes later he was reluctantly putting the same dirty clothes back on a clean body. He would have asked her whether she wanted him to bring her any breakfast, but she was asleep again, her hand across her face as if to ward off a blow.

Mozza woke himself with his watch alarm an hour before dawn, and spent it thawing himself out before a rekindled fire. His feet seemed no worse than the previous morning, which he supposed was the most he could have hoped for. After boiling water for tea he doused the fire, cleared up his camp-site, and sipped from the cone as the dawn lit the roof of the forest above him.

The first hour's walk had him following the lower

tree line round the upper slopes of a wide, moorland valley. The sky was not as clear as on the previous day, but there were still large patches of blue between the floating cumulus. The stream flowed into the valley from the west, and Mozza followed it back up into the forest, climbing alongside it for about three miles, until the trees suddenly cleared and he found himself confronting a large, silver-blue lake, surrounded on all sides by snow-capped hills. Two birds that looked suspiciously like eagles were drawing lazy circles in the sky above.

The lake stretched about six miles from east to west, between half a mile and a mile from north to south. It had an air of utter stillness, and working his way along its southern shore Mozza felt his mind settling into some sort of ease for the first time since the fire-fight at the airbase.

Every now and then he came across evidence of past human activity: a crumbling section of fence, a burnt-out fishing lodge, wooden piles that had once supported a jetty. The land had rejected them all, sent their creators scurrying back to the comfort of cities.

Almost halfway down the lake a narrow promontory leading out into the lake looked custom-made for fishing. Mozza cut himself a rod, attached his line, and impaled several berries from an overhanging tree on the hook. Then he cast the line and settled down to wait, keeping watchful eyes and ears on the world around him.

He did not have long to wait. Within a minute a medium-sized trout had taken the lure and been landed. Mozza cut it open and dutifully examined the contents of its stomach to check what bait he should be using, but it hardly seemed to matter. Another trout almost leapt out onto the shore to join him.

The temptation to cook them there and then was strong, but self-discipline prevailed. He walked on, allowing himself to dwell for the first time on the events of the night before last. He supposed Brookes and Stanley were dead, and though he could not say he had ever felt close to either of them, they had both been damn good soldiers.

Whatever that meant, an inner voice murmured.

He had always assumed that he could kill someone when the need arose, that when the moment came to turn the exercises and simulations and techniques into real combat he would find that switch which released him from moral inhibitions. Now he was not so sure. He had learnt silent killing techniques at Hereford like everyone else, and he was as technically adept as Stanley had been. But he was not sure whether he could have cut that guard's throat the way Stanley had.

And he was no longer sure he wanted to be able to do it. Shooting someone in self-defence was one thing; taking someone out in cold blood was another. But what did that mean? That he needed to look for another line of work? Maybe he did.

The road ran in alternating curves along the upper slope of a huge valley. To their right, at least 20 miles away, the far slopes were bathed in light, but the sun had yet to reach the depths in between. Almost directly ahead of them, and also far distant, a town nestled at the head of either a lake or an arm of the sea. 'Puerto Natales,' Ben said. 'We're about seven miles away from El Turbio,' he added, examining the map again. 'Sounds like a bandit who named himself after an engine. Anyway, I think we can start looking for somewhere to turn off.'

'Good idea,' Razor said dryly, 'but a bit on the late side.'

Ben looked up.

'About half a mile ahead,' Razor explained. 'You'll see it when we round the next curve.'

'Trouble?' Ben murmured. It was not really a question.

'A road block. A couple of vehicles and a few Johnny Gauchos.'

The next curve brought it back into view. A military lorry and a jeep had been arranged in an inverted V at a particularly favourable location. On one side of the road a solid rock wall prevented the block's circumvention; on the other was a precipitous grassy slope.

About a dozen troops seemed to be rapidly organizing themselves at the approach of their car.

'How wide do you think that gap is?' Razor asked conversationally, his foot pressing down on the accelerator.

Ben looked in disbelief at the fast-approaching roadblock. Two hundred yards, 150 ... 'About a foot,' he said, 'for Christ's sake ...'

'Not the one in the middle,' Razor said calmly, as the troops began raising their weapons, and his right hand eased down on the steering wheel.

Ben watched the valley loom towards them, hardly noticing the bullets which made two holes in the windscreen and passed between their heads, and felt his neck almost yanked from his body as the car surfed past the outer edge of the jeep, its right-side wheels scrambling for a hold and seeming to spend an eternity in finding one.

'That gap,' Razor said calmly.

'Jesus Christ,' Ben said.

The roadblock was shrinking in the rear mirror, but he did not slacken his speed. They went down one long, sweeping curve and then another.

'Trees,' Razor said.

A quarter of a mile ahead of them the road descended into the fringes of a coniferous forest. From their bird's-eye view they could see where logging operations had exposed a number of bald patches in the tree cover.

'Time to melt into them,' Ben said.

They were half a mile into the forest when Razor found what he was looking for — a tight curve over a steep and already logged slope. 'This'll do,' he said, slamming on the brakes, and reversing back up the hill.

'Out,' he told Ben, who dutifully obliged.

Razor accelerated forward. The VW was going about 20 miles per hour when he slammed the clutch into neutral and hurled himself out onto the road. He rolled over several times and scrambled to his feet, just in time to see the car disappear over the edge.

Ben was already running down the slope to his right, headed for the cover of the trees, and Razor raced after him, listening to the VW's passage, which sounded rather like a large animal breaking through underbrush. It ended suddenly with a satisfying explosion.

'I thought they were supposed to be indestructible,' Razor said breathlessly, as he caught up with Ben some 20 yards inside the trees.

'This is far enough,' Ben told him.

The two men put tree trunks between themselves and the road and waited for the pursuit to catch up. It was less than half a minute behind them. A jeep jammed with troops pulled up on the bend above, and voices floated down through the clear morning air. The word '*loco*' seemed much in evidence to Razor, but he might have been imagining it.

Whoever was in command showed no urgent inclination to send anyone down after the VW, let alone mount a proper search. Taking one curve on two wheels had obviously implanted the possibility of such an accident in the Argentinian commander's mind. As far as he was concerned, the SAS men were dead until proved otherwise.

The lorry arrived, picked up all but two of the men, and continued on its way.

The two SAS men breathed a sigh of relief. Though they were confident they could have outrun the opposition in rough country if necessary, a stroll in the sunshine was certainly more fun without armed pursuit.

Above them the pair of soldiers left behind with the jeep talked and smoked a leisurely cigarette before reluctantly clambering over the rim of the slope and disappearing from sight. Ben gave them a minute and then went up to check that there was no radio in the jeep.

'No,' he told Razor on his return. 'Chile, here we come,' he added, examining the map.

'More haste is a friend indeed,' Razor said wisely.

After eating breakfast Docherty stretched out on the bed beside Isabel, set the alarm on his watch and slept for four hours. He awoke feeling more tired than when he had gone to bed, and took another shower. Isabel was still asleep, but her face seemed more childlike, more at ease. She was about Chrissie's size, he thought, maybe an inch taller. He took the money from her shoulder bag and went out looking for new clothes for both of them.

Calafate looked like any tourist town out of season – half-asleep. Most of the few shops seem closed, either for the weekend or the off season, but on Calle 25 de Mayo he managed to find one selling clothes and camping equipment. The prices seemed extortionate, but he consoled himself with the thought that MI6 was paying. He bought a pair of jeans, two T-shirts, a sweater, spare socks and underwear for himself, and a couple of T-shirts and a sweater for Isabel. She already had a change of clothes, and if she wanted anything else one of them could always come back. He had only spent a quarter of the money.

He stopped off for a hamburger and coffee at an empty café, and watched the street through the window. He had not seen a policeman or soldier since leaving the hotel, and wondered how much longer they would be safe in Calafate. He guessed the Argentinians would be concentrating their search in the immediate area of Rio Gallegos, at least until they had reason to look elsewhere. Eventually though, they would connect the woman the guard had seen to the missing Isabel, and then the hunt for her car would begin. Luckily the car park of their hotel was out of sight from any road. They would have to be doing a rigorous check of all the hotels to find it.

He wondered how Razor and Ben were getting on and looked at his watch. It was midday – there was a good chance they would have reached the border by this time. The Cup Final was kicking off too, he realized, smiling to himself.

He finished the coffee and paid the cheque to a friendly young woman. He liked Latin America, he decided. Mexico had not been a one-off.

Back at the hotel he left the clothes and went out again. They needed an escape route, or preferably two – one to use in their own sweet time and one for emergencies. The tourist office was closed, but maps of the town and the province were displayed in its window. He spent ten minutes drawing rough copies and fending off offers of help from the locals.

Then he followed the town map to the Plaza San Martín, and walked uphill to the top of the long Calle Perito Moreno. From there he had a breathtaking view of the distant Andes, and the blue-green Lago Argentina stretching away from the town towards the mountains' feet.

It occurred to him for the first time that one way out of Calafate was by boat.

Isabel woke in the empty room of the Hospedaje del Glaciar and thought for one horrible moment that she was back in a cell. It was the light, she decided, or the lack of it. Her cell at the Naval Mechanical School had been dazzlingly bright with the fluorescent light on, perpetual twilight with it off. There had been no real night – only nightmares.

She climbed slowly off the bed, expecting a sharper pain than the one she received. It was healing well, she decided. There was nothing wrong with her body's recuperative powers. By the next day there would be little more than stiffness.

She pulled one of the curtains, and found the lake stretching away from her towards a distant line of blue hills. As she turned, the pile of bags by the door caught her attention, and she walked slowly across to investigate. He had been clothes-shopping! And for her, too. The thick sweater, a deep burgundy red, would suit her. She carried it across to the mirror and held it up in front of her.

Christ, she looked a wreck, she thought. Her eyes were like bruises in a ghost's face. She looked like someone who had just been shot, she thought, and laughed. It transformed her face. She was feeling good, she realized with surprise. Despite it all she was feeling good. Something somewhere had snapped. Some exorcism had taken place.

She wondered where the Englishman was now. Docherty, that was his name. She tried it out loud: 'Dokker-tee'. And he was a Scotsman, not an Englishman. They were touchy about such things. And she liked him.

Christ, what was she thinking? She had known him for less than twenty-four hours, and all she knew about the man was that he thought well on his feet, killed people efficiently and seemed to possess that streak of mad gallantry which often went with being one of the most unreconstructed macho bastards on the planet.

Just like Francisco, she thought, and she had forgiven him everything because of his beauty and his politics and his ability to be tender. Well, Mr Docherty was not beautiful, his politics were likely to be conservative-verging-on-fascist, and she would probably never know how tender he could be.

But she did like him. There was something about

him, some sadness maybe, which seemed incredibly human.

It was probably the snoring that had woken him, Wacko thought. He was in what looked like a hospital room, and directly in front of him, seated beside the door, a guard with an automatic rifle was dozing with his mouth wide open.

Wacko tried to move, almost cried out with pain, and seemed to lose consciousness again for just a few seconds. He felt really weird, he realized. Maybe some sort of drug had been pumped into him, or maybe it was just one of the consequences of being shot wherever it was he had been. The chest, he thought. He tried to examine his arm for needle marks but the room started to swim, and he had to close his eyes tight.

The next time he awoke – whether minutes or hours later was impossible to tell – it was to hear voices. There were two men, either standing in the doorway or just outside. Wacko kept his eyes closed and tried to concentrate on what they were saying. One voice was soft and one rasping, like two instruments alternating solos in a piece of chamber music. They were talking about someone or something named Solanille, about someone or other looking everywhere, about a woman – a 'mystery woman'.

'And what is to be done with this one?' the rasping voice asked. Wacko thought he could feel eyes glancing towards him.

'Nothing,' the soft voice said, causing Wacko to clench his fist in elation under the sheet. 'The war is probably lost,' the man said, his voice even softer than before, 'and who knows how the people will react . . .'

'But this is an Englishman. A terrorist. What do the people care about . . .'

'You are being naïve, Carlos. If the people turn on the Junta then it will be a lottery for those of us in the security services. But one thing is certain – the cleaner our hands appear to be the more chance we shall have of keeping our positions. I do not want my name on some list the English Ambassador to the UN reads out, just when a new government in Buenos Aires is looking for scapegoats in the security services.'

'I see what you mean,' Carlos agreed.

'Good.'

'So we wait for the war to be over, one way or another.'

'We hand him back to the Air Force, him and his friend from Rio Grande.' The soft-voiced one grunted, apparently with amusement. 'If by some miracle we win the war, then we can always ask for him back.'

The voices went on, but Wacko, unable to hold his concentration any longer, drifted back into unconsciousness. The next time he awoke Hedge was sitting beside him, apparently dressed in pyjamas.

'Welcome to St Gaucho's,' the big man said.

The sun was high in the clear blue sky when Razor and Ben emerged from the trees and saw, half a mile below them, a line of widely spaced white posts laid across the vast, wild slope, fading into the distance.

'It must be the border,' Ben said.

'Don't see what else it could be,' Razor agreed.

There was no sign of troops, nor of any other

humans. But for the line of white posts there was no sign that men had ever walked there before.

They moved down cautiously, looking for any signs of a minefield, without really expecting to find any. At a point directly between two of the posts Razor took a large symbolic step. 'One second you're a soldier at war, the next you're a tourist,' he proclaimed.

'Or an internee,' Ben corrected him.

'As long as there's a hot meal involved,' Razor said.

They walked on, their steps a little lighter for having crossed the border, but it was another four hours before they came upon a rough track. They followed it down into an idyllic little valley, where a stream danced happily over stones beneath lovely cypresses, and a real road wound out of sight to left and right.

Less than ten minutes had passed when a farmer responded to Razor's optimistic thumb, and stopped to give them a lift. He chatted merrily about nothing in particular, but seemed entirely devoid of curiosity as to who they were. He also failed to shed any light on the outcome of the Cup Final.

He drove them the five miles into Puerto Natales, a small town whose houses all seemed to be made of either wood or corrugated iron. At Razor's request they were dropped outside the Post Office, which happened to face the town's main square.

Ben sat in the latter while Razor entered the former, and stretched his Spanish to the utmost in a long but ultimately successful attempt to make a reversed-charge telephone call to the British Embassy in Santiago.

'Who shall I say is calling?' the Chilean official asked.

'Trooper Wilkinson of the SAS,' Razor told him. 'We're a sort of travelling show,' he added helpfully.

The Embassy answered immediately, as if they had been waiting for the call. Once Razor had explained his and Ben's geographical and pecuniary situations, he was told to wait in the square until a man named Lawson came to collect the two of them. It might be several hours before he could get there, and perhaps not before morning. In the meantime, somewhat unrealistically, they should try not to attract any attention to themselves.

Razor went back to Ben, and the two of them sat side by side on a bench, in their filthy Gore-tex jackets and camouflage trousers, staring at the statue of some Chilean general.

'Fuck this for a laugh,' Razor said after a few minutes. 'Let's try and change the Argie money, eat and drink ourselves into a stupor, find some nice girls and have a fucking ball.'

'As long as we don't attract any attention to ourselves,' Ben said.

'Goes without saying,' Razor agreed.

Docherty thought Isabel's face looked anxious when he let himself back into the room. 'There's no sign of the opposition,' he said quickly, and then noticed that she was wearing the sweater he had bought for her.

'It seems to fit,' he said. 'Is the colour OK?'

'It's lovely,' she said.

He felt pleased.

'But where have you been since?' she asked.

'Here and there. Exploring the town.'

267

'Don't . . . I mean, I'm not telling you what to do, but don't you think it would be better if we stayed out of sight.'

He took no offence. 'Yes and no,' he said. 'I wanted to make sure the car was as out of sight as possible, without actually pushing it into the lake. And I always like to know where the back door is, so to speak, just in case someone comes knocking at the front.' He grinned at her. 'Other than that, yes, we should stay out of sight.'

She sighed. 'Point taken.'

'Let me ask you a question,' he said. 'How long do you think it will be safe to stay here?'

She took time to think about her answer, which was the one of the things he most liked about her. 'Does anyone know we came this way?'

'Not that I know of, but . . .' He shrugged. 'You never know when someone's looking out through the lace curtains.'

'If they've lost us, then I'd guess several days,' she said, 'but there's no guarantee.'

'Of course not. Another question: have you ever done any mountain hiking?'

'Are you kidding?' I grew up in Ushuaia. I climbed every mountain in the National Park before I was sixteen.'

'Great. Well, this is the plan.' He brought out the map he had copied, and outlined their escape route. 'But you'll need all the strength you can muster,' he added. Somehow, going over it all with her had only emphasized how hard it might turn out to be.

'Don't worry about me,' she said, 'I've always been strong as an ox.'

'You don't look like one.'

She smiled. 'Just give me one more day.'

Mozza had spent the previous night camped in a convenient cave, just above the tree line on the northern slope of another range of miniature mountains. Puma tracks by the cave mouth had made him feel slightly ambivalent. While he would have loved to see one up close in the wild, he did not feel much like having to fight off an angry cat whose home he had stolen. Still, there were no recent droppings, and the two baked trout had been tasty enough to take his mind off everything else. He had slept like a child, perhaps in unconscious recognition of the rigours of the day to come.

The mountains were less than 3500 feet high, he reckoned, but the top three hundred were wreathed in permanent snow, and they looked just like the Alps through the wrong end of a telescope. More to the point, since the range ran almost north to south, he had no choice but to cross it.

Fortified at first light by another hot meal and drink, he was quickly on his way, climbing steadily up across the bare mountain towards the snowline. The temperature seemed to drop steadily despite the rising sun, and once he was into the snow his feet started to ache, and his eyes to blink. The going was not difficult, and he pressed on for the best part of another hour without ever seeming to be any nearer the summit, his vision assuming a pink hue which steadily darkened towards red.

He forced himself to stop, eyes closed, feeling his feet turning into blocks of ice, fighting off a rising sense of panic. 'Lynsey, Lynsey, Lynsey,' he said to himself. He visualized her face at the door, the smile, the embrace. He then tried walking with the PNGs on, keeping his eyes dangerously closed on stretches that seemed straightforward.

After what seemed an age he reached the top of the pass. Taking off the PNGs he could see, far in the distance and way down below, another large lake stretching away into the haze.

It was almost noon. He took another two biscuits and two more squares of chocolate, promised himself a cup of tea beneath the snowline, and started down. His feet were now sending out severe shooting pains, but somehow he knew the worst was over.

An hour later the snow gave way to alpine meadow, and he followed an icy stream down a steep, winding valley towards the occasionally visible lake. There was no wood for making a fire, but once out of the snow his feet had held their own, and he was confident he could reach the water before the sun disappeared behind him.

He was still some way from the lake when the noise started percolating into his consciousness. It grew steadily in volume as he approached, a sound somewhere between braying and squawking, like a football crowd full of angry donkeys.

It was only when he turned the last corner of the valley that he saw the source: hundreds upon hundreds of penguins were spread across the beach, walking up and down, apparently talking to each other.

They hardly seemed to notice his arrival. He turned the corner of the cliff, and found he had underestimated their numbers. There seemed to be thousands of them, spread as far as he could see up the lakeside beach, all honking up a storm.

Except that penguins only lived by the sea, he reminded himself. He had read it in Hannah's book of animals before he left. And if this was the sea then he was in Chile. He sniffed at the cold air to make sure, and smelt the salt. He was safe. He would be going home.

Docherty was woken by church bells the following morning, and decided that the chair he had slept in must have been engineered by a sadist. Every muscle in his body seemed stiff.

Isabel seemed much stronger for a good night's sleep, and the two of them had breakfast together in the almost empty hotel dining-room. Rosa continued to treat them as though they were favoured relatives, which perhaps had something to do with Isabel's fictional guidebook. In any case, her non-stop chatter about herself, the hotel and the town revealed no new cause for alarm.

Docherty spent most of the day spending MI6's money. He had been half afraid the camping shop would be closed, but as if engaged in a desperate effort to squeeze the last drop from the tourist trade, its doors were defiantly open. He purchased a tent, sleeping bags, footwear for Isabel, a pack for carrying it all – and everything else they would need for several days' hiking in subarctic conditions.

All day he kept an eye out for any sign of trouble, but the town seemed as becalmed as the waters of its lake. Newspaper headlines suggested great victories in the Malvinas, but to judge from the locals' faces they believed it as little as Docherty did.

Isabel stayed in the hotel, gathering her strength and letting her mind wander. If they got away, then where would she go? What would she do? What did she make of this man?

They ate dinner in the dining-room, and he talked about the months he had spent in Mexico. She found herself wondering more and more why this man did what he did, and then she remembered how and who he had been during that long night in Rio Gallegos. Some people, she thought, just do what they do because they know how good they are at doing it.

Back upstairs he did all but the last-minute packing, ramming more into the backpack than she would have thought possible. When he had finished, it seemed to weighed a ton, but was apparently half the weight he usually carried.

'We're ready,' he said, as much to himself as her. 'And the more sleep we get, the better,' he added.

'I think you should sleep in the bed tonight,' she said.

'OK,' he said.

'I mean with me,' she said.

'Yeah,' he said, making sure the door was locked. 'Don't worry, I'll keep my distance.'

She was silent for a moment. Then she stepped across to meet him, and put her two hands on his shoulder, and kissed him softly on the lips. 'I mean, I want us to make love,' she said. 'It doesn't have to be now. I just wanted to tell you.'

'Oh,' he said.

'If you want to,' she added.

'I've wanted to since the first moment I saw you in that hotel lobby,' he said. 'But you're not properly mended yet . . .'

'Oh, I can manage,' she said, easing her good arm around his neck. They kissed, first gently, then with a slowly growing passion that neither had known for many years.

'I shall need some help undressing,' she said.

'Look no further,' Docherty said mildly, caressing her hair. She carefully straightened her arms, allowing him to pull the sweater and T-shirt up over her head, and he managed to unfasten the bra with an ease which was unique in his experience.

He leaned down to kiss her breasts, noticing the faded scars of burns across them, and felt an intermingling of desire and pity which almost choked him.

She pulled him back up. 'They're old scars,' she said softly, and applied her fingers to his belt buckle.

After making love they lay talking in the large bed, half-conscious of the growing silence around them as hotel and town went to sleep.

'Tell me about you,' she said. 'You know all about me.'

'No I don't,' he said. 'I know you were a revolutionary, and you were captured and tortured, and your family managed to get you out of the country somehow. And that you agreed to work for MI6 because of your hatred for the Junta. But none of that prepared me for who you are.'

'So who am I?' she asked wryly.

'You're someone who couldn't shoot the man who sent you to the torturers . . .'

'I know. I could kill that man at the door, who I

had never seen in my life before, but I couldn't kill Solanille.'

'Your finger could have pulled the trigger. Your head knew how to give the order. Your heart just didn't want it done.' He smiled. 'In the films they always say that's what separates us from them.'

'In the films they still believe in good and evil.'

'And so do you.'

She smiled. 'Yes, I do. Outside myself I do.'

'And you make love like an angel,' he added, running his fingers through her hair and feeling himself beginning to stir once more.

'You're changing the subject,' she said. 'And you still haven't told me anything about yourself.'

'It's a sad story,' he said.

'It can't be that sad.'

'Why not? Do you think . . .'

'Because you make love like an angel too,' she interrupted him, running her hand down his stomach. 'You can tell me the sad story later,' she said.

An hour before dawn they left the hotel, walked swiftly down to the lake and along to the small motor boat Docherty had selected for their journey. A crescent moon hung in the sky, casting a thin light across the waters, but there were no witnesses to watch their departure. Docherty rowed them out into the lake and past the first headland, only engaging the outboard motor when they were about half a mile from the town.

The darkness began to dissipate, and then suddenly, or so it seemed, the snowy peaks of the mountains ahead were ignited by the still invisible sun, and seemed to burn with white fire.

Through the morning they passed down the blue-green lake, the wall of the southern Andes drawing ever nearer. They turned south where the lake divided, the shimmering wall of the Moreno Glacier visible in the distance, the cracking of its ice highly audible across the water. Just before noon Docherty grounded the boat in a shallow cove on the lake's south-western shore. He disembarked Isabel, himself and the pack, and then shoved the now-floating boat back out into the lake. For a moment it sat stationary on the water and then, as if called by its unfortunate owner in Calafate, started drifting back the way they had come.

Once Docherty had checked the map the two fugitives started slowly climbing the valley behind the cove, Isabel ahead, the laden SAS man behind. She looked strong, he thought, and he hoped to God she was.

That night they pitched their tent a good way above the lake, and discovered that Docherty had chosen the sleeping bags well – once unzipped they could be united to make a double.

The next day they resumed their climb, moving no faster than Isabel could easily manage, and stopping well before dark to set up camp as efficiently as the conditions warranted. Then they cooked, talked, made love and slept. The rest of the world had been left with the drifting boat below.

The following day was much the same. The sky stayed clear and the temperature dropped, but now they were more than halfway to their goal. And sure enough, soon after midday they crested what proved to be the final ridge, and found themselves looking down a long valley running into the west. They were standing on the border.

'Out of one fascist dictatorship and into another,' Isabel said cheerfully.

And out of one life and into another, she dared herself to hope.

Epilogue

The crew of the Sea King managed to sustain themselves for nine days in the Chilean wilderness, and only decided to hand themselves over to the authorities when a party of local trekkers blundered into their camp.

They were flown from Punta Arenas to Santiago, where they gave a press conference on Wednesday 26 May. 'We were on sea patrol when we experienced engine failure due to adverse weather conditions,' they explained. 'It was not possible to return to our ship in these conditions. We therefore took refuge in the nearest neutral country.'

The few people who believed this story did not include anyone in political or military service with the British or Argentinian governments.

By this time Razor and Ben were already on board a plane above the Atlantic, headed home to a discreet heroes' welcome and two weeks' immediate leave. Ben took the overnight train north with an anxious heart, not knowing how he was going to tell Morag that he had decided his future lay with the SAS. He did not want to lose her, but if she forced him to choose, then that would have to be his choice.

It was a beautiful morning in Fort William, and

she met him off the train with the news that she had taken the afternoon off. This was surprising enough in itself, but one look at her face and he knew that she had missed him much more she had expected. They took the local train to Glenfinnan and walked up across the heather to a place above the viaduct, the famous statue of Bonnie Prince Charlie a distant spot far below, and made love beneath the blue sky, the sun warm on their skin.

Afterwards, knowing what he had to say to her, Ben felt almost guilty. But it was she who first broached the subject of their future, announcing that she was withdrawing her ultimatum. 'My father says you'd be a fool to leave the Army at the moment,' she added, 'with unemployment rising so fast.'

He looked at her, wondering how he could get across what he felt about it all. 'It what's I *do*,' he said helplessly.

On arriving back at Heathrow, Razor had found to his delight that the Cup Final replay was scheduled for that evening. It was not exactly a good game, and jet lag had added its contribution to his overall exhaustion, but he managed to stay awake for the sight of a Tottenham player holding up the Cup for the second year running. And next season, with their two Argies back in midfield, the sky would be the limit.

His mum was certainly pleased to see Razor back – in fact she hardly seemed to stop fussing over him from morning till night. Then he overheard her end of a telephone conversation, and thought he understood why. That evening he announced he was going out with Corinna – which was true – and that it was about time his mother found herself a man to look after her. He was fed up feeling guilty for being away so much, he said.

And then she told him about the new man in her life, grinning like a schoolgirl.

Razor felt really happy for her, and could hardly stop smiling all evening, at least until Corinna found another use for his lips. Familiarity makes the heart grow fonder, he thought, as they wrestled each other into her bed.

In the third week of June, the week that followed the final Argentinian surrender in Port Stanley, there were memorial services for both Stanley and Brookes, in West Bromwich and Hereford respectively. Bryan Weighell and Bill Hemmings attended both of them, as did many of their regimental comrades.

At the end of the service for Brookes, Weighell asked Hemmings if the number of Super Etendards in service with the Argentinian Air Force had ever been finally established.

'Not with complete certainty,' the Welshman admitted. 'But every indication we have is that there were only five of them.'

'And they took out three,' Weighell murmured to himself.

'They did that. And the other two sank the *Atlantic Conveyor* and the *Coventry* four days later. God knows what damage they might have done with all five still available.'

'They'll get some recognition, of course,' Weighell said, 'but no one will know what it was for. Which always seems a pity, somehow.'

In the same week, in the northern Argentinian town of

Metán, a funeral Mass was held for the repose of Raul Vergara's soul. His body had never been recovered from the sea, but his spirit could be seen reflected in the upturned faces of his mother and father, brother and sisters, sweetheart and friends.

Later, back at the Vergara house, amid the expected protestations of sorrow and pride, the anger that now lay so close to the surface of Argentinian life was occasionally expressed. Bitter voices were heard asking how, after such a defeat and so many lost, the Generals could still cling to power.

A few days later Wacko and Hedge were dispatched for home via the Uruguayan capital, Montevideo. It was more than a month since their capture and Wacko felt good as new, but Hedge knew his knee would never be the same again.

Their treatment, first in Rio Gallegos and then in Buenos Aires, had improved as the Argentinian Army's fortunes had declined. Garbled reports of the negotiations for their release had reached them in the suburban villa where they were confined, but the government official's arrival that morning with the news of their imminent departure had come as a very pleasant surprise. A long drive to the docks had afforded them their first and last view of 'South America's Paris', and now they were leaning against the rail of a ferry across the River Plate, looking out on the scene of the famous battle.

Hedge had seen the film about five times as a kid, and had always secretly wanted the Germans to win. He supposed that that was because their captain seemed more English than the English. He stared out at the rolling waves and wondered if the film had been made here. He doubted it. In fact, they had probably shot most of it in one of those big tanks in the old film studios.

Despite the gammy knee, he had to admit to feeling pretty good. During the weeks in captivity, and particularly through those first uncertain hours and days, he knew he had held himself together well. He was glad to be going home, but he had no regrets about coming. He reckoned his father would have been proud of him.

Wacko was feeling much the same sense of achievement, and even looking forward to seeing Anne. The letters she had written since receiving news of his capture had seemed to come from a much more loving person than the one he remembered. Maybe there was still something there to build on, or maybe they would find it better to just go their separate ways. It seemed not to matter as much as it had.

Mozza did not arrive back in England until some time after Razor, Ben, Docherty and Isabel. His penguin colony had certainly been on Chilean soil, but a particularly remote part of it, and it took him the best part of forty-eight hours to find his first native. This fisherman gave him a lift to Dawson Island, and from there he got another to Punta Arenas, which was still discussing Razor and Ben's blow-out the weekend before. Mozza finally reached Heathrow on the first day of June.

Like Razor and Ben, he was given a fortnight's immediate leave, and the homecoming in Manchester proved everything he had hoped for. Lynsey's smile and open arms were exactly as he had visualized them in the forest on Tierra del Fuego, and every day for a week he had to tell Hannah the story of how he had met all the penguins on the beach.

His nights, though, were not so kind. For several in a row he had a dream of falling through a pool of blood, and each time he awoke in a cold sweat with Lynsey's worried face looking into his. Eventually he told her what had happened on the Rio Grande airfield, or at least enough of it to give her some understanding of what he was dreaming about.

She just held him tight until he fell asleep in her arms, but the next day, as they watched Hannah playing in the park sandpit, she said she had been thinking about it and wanted to say something. 'Maybe the dream is trying to tell you something,' she began, 'maybe you weren't meant to be a soldier, no matter how good you feel about being one.'

He turned his innocent eyes towards her. 'Why, what's wrong with me?'

'Nothing, nothing at all. Maybe it's what's right with you. People who wear their hearts on their sleeve can't cut themselves off from what they're doing. And you're like that. It's what makes you such a wonderful man.'

'I don't think I'm so wonderful,' he said. 'But maybe you're right about the rest.'

Isabel Fuentes and Liam McCall were sitting in his local, just round the corner from the church, waiting for Docherty to come back from visiting his mother.

'I've been thinking about who really won the war,' Isabel said.

'What do you mean?' the priest asked.

'I get the news from Argentina now,' she said, 'and it really looks like the military's days are numbered.

The elections will be held – everyone seems sure of it. My country will get a good government out of this war, or at least a better one. And at some point they will have to go back and look at what was done in the Dirty War. The Mothers of the Disappeared will accept nothing less, and now the people are behind them.'

She took a sip of her beer. 'Oh, I'm not saying that everything is perfect there, or that the torturers will all be punished. They won't be. But some will, and it will make it harder for the others to show their faces. Argentina is a better place for losing the war. Whereas England . . .' She sighed, and reached again for her glass.

'I know what you mean,' Liam said. 'The woman was on her way out, and now we've probably got her for the next ten years. And at the rate she's going there won't be much left of the country I used to love by the time she's finished.'

They both sat in silence for a moment.

'And what are you and Jamie intending to do?' he asked eventually. 'If you don't mind my asking.'

'We don't know,' she said simply. 'We were talking about it the other night, and we decided that there was only one thing we were both qualified for, and that was creating mayhem.'

Liam grinned. 'Is Jamie going to stay with the SAS?'

'I don't know,' Isabel replied. 'But you can ask him yourself,' she added, her dark eyes lighting up.

Docherty wended his way through the tables and sat down, taking her hand in his.

'We were just discussing your future,' Liam said.

'Oh aye, which future's that?'

'That's what we were trying to work out.'

Docherty opened a bag of crisps and handed it round. 'I've got two months left of a three-year term,' he said. 'When the time comes I'll decide whether I think this is a country worth serving. And if the answer is yes, I'll ask this woman here if she agrees with me. And if she does, then . . . who knows? Maybe we'll live in a bungalow outside Hereford and raise children.'

'Or maybe we'll go and create mayhem somewhere else,' Isabel said.